OPIATE WARRIOR

Using Mindful Medically Assisted Treatment to Successfully Combat Opiate Use Disorder

Linear Vision Publishing

Roseanna Andrews

OPIATE WARRIOR

Using Mindful Medically Assisted Treatment to Successfully Combat Opiate Use Disorder

Linear Vision Publishing

Opiate Warrior Copyright © 2020 by Linear Vision Publishing.

All Rights Reserved. No part of this book may be reproduced in any form or by any electronic or mechanical means including information storage and retrieval systems, without permission in writing from the author. The only exception is by a viewer, who may quote short excerpts in a review.

This book is a work of nonfiction self-help. The author of this book does not dispense medical advice or prescribe the use of any technique as a form of treatment for any physical or medical problems without the advice of a physician, either directly or indirectly. The intent of the author is only to offer information of a general nature to help you in your quest for emotional and spiritual wellbeing. In the event you use any of the information in this book for yourself, the author and the publisher assume no responsibility for your actions.

Printed in the United States of America
First Printed: March 2020
Cover designed by Laura Muhaxheri

SBN-979-8-3906-3801-9

BENEFITING THE GREATER GOOD OF OUR PLANET
BY EXPANDING HUMAN CONSCIOUSNESS
OUR SOLE PURPOSE IS TO HELP YOU FIND YOUR SOUL PURPOSE

I lovingly dedicate this book to my amazing parents and beautiful, precious daughters, who taught me that love really can move mountains.

Keep your thoughts positive because your thoughts become your words. Keep your words positive because your words become your behavior. Keep your behavior positive because your behavior becomes your habits.

- MAHATMA GHANDHI

Once we were given the gift of creation,
with the light of the stars to guide our way home.
Yet with all of our time here, the layers of illusions,
just blocked memory, of that which once was.
The seed of truth that was planted so very deep in our souls,
waiting for a prayer or a wake-up call from God,
to glimpse some truth,
that reminds us, what we are really made of.
Maybe it is the singing of that strange star catcher song,
or the net of creation, thrown across the skies,
that can retrieve us and bring us home.
Did it come from some strange vision,
Or a dream sent as a reminder so we can see?
What it was that called to us, so long ago,
and really transformed us to believe.
The golden chisel of Earth's temple.
A reflection that is seen in our souls.
A chance to dress as God in form,
with a hidden key that we all know.
And somewhere the door to paradise was left open,
and so, we can be set free,
to dwell in the houses of the holy or stay in the world of dreams.
Until we hear the hark the Harold angels bring,
with that breath of creation,
that holds this inner truth alive in everything.
And perhaps some part of us, still remembers,
what we really came here for.
And we see past the illusions and find the power to see the vision of Heaven's shores.
And we reach beyond the lifetimes it takes
to wake up to the call of God,
and find out what was meant to be.
And we leave the illusions behind,
as we find the trail of secrets and hidden clues.
With this great gift of Divine love and Being,
that lives in the soul of me and you.

-DR. WAYNE W. DYER – THE GIFT OF CREATION

Table of Contents

Introduction	xiii
Preface	xxi

CHAPTER I
Opium's Origin 1

CHAPTER II
Rise of Western Medicine 9

CHAPTER III
Addiction's Creation Story 27

CHAPTER IV
Opiated Opioids 33

CHAPTER V
Love is not Tough 41

CHAPTER VI
Mindful Medicine 53

CHAPTER VII
Returning to Consciousness 65
    POWER OF THE WORDS "I AM" 76
    LOST GOSPELS OF THOMAS 77

CHAPTER VIII
Reflective Power 85

CHAPTER IX
Life in the Fast(ing) Lane 103

CHAPTER X
Ascended Masters and Spirit Guides 113
    MEETING YOUR SPIRIT GUIDE MEDITATION 113

CHAPTER XI
Vibrational Frequencies   121

CHAPTER XII
30-Day Path to Freedom + Personal Progress Calendar   141
  SEA SALT CLEANSING BATH   *150*
  BREATHING EXERCISE FOR RELIEVING ANXIETY   *153*
  HEALING BENEFITS OF GOLD   *155*
  AYURVEDIC ART OF COLOR THERAPY   *159*
  30 DAYS TO FREEDOM MIRROR EXERCISE   *163*
30-DAY PERSONAL PROGRESS CALENDAR   *177*
SELF-HELP RESOURCES   *179*
RECOMMENDED READING   *181*

Introduction

Who is he? Who is this man that strides as if he rules the Earth, and all those that inhabit it? He tells me he sees all, and therefore holds the answers to all the secrets and mysteries that ever were, or ever will be. He tells me I am only a child and that I cannot hold myself up on my own two feet without my mother's grasp. What he does not know is she has only remained by my side to stabilize her own balance. He does not know she needs me more than I have ever needed her. Now he is the king of our world. How did this happen?

Addiction is a terrible thing. It can wipe down entire cities with just a single taste. It can ruin relationships, destroy families, and reveal undiscovered worlds. I have not experimented with drugs, although I have experienced the power of addiction through another woman's eyes, somebody I love very dearly. She had sacrificed herself to the crazed world of opium eaters and delusional needle lovers. I was too blind to see the truth. Too distracted with my own pathetic attempt to remain optimistic. I do not know exactly when it began. All I know is that he was the cause. My family and I spent years building our new life from scratch, and he willingly came along to light the match that would eventually burn all our hard work to the ground.

I remember walking to the store with my mother and sister. We passed a strange house that was leaking the smell of burnt rubber. "Black tar heroin," my mother said. "Never go anywhere near that stuff. It will ruin your life. Let's get out of here girls. That smell is making me sick." It is ironic really, and even funny, a great lesson given from one's own hypocrisy. I was introduced to him that day. He came to me through my mother's wisdom. I did not know at the time he would eventually take her as another one of his victims.

Needles have been my phobia for as long as I can remember. Even at doctor appointments, about six people would have to hold me down to give me my shots. They did not even hurt, just a prick. I do not know why I feared them so much. Maybe it was just the idea of a sharp object injecting strange substances into my body. Why they scared me does not matter; it is the fact that she knew I feared them. She knew, and she still invited them into our home. I remember a strange man I did not like. He would leave them on the stove and in the bathroom. Soon enough, I would be checking the couch before I sat down in fear of being poked. Imagine that. Confined in a space surrounded by your worst nightmare. Having to fear accidentally being pricked by something so dangerous, so evil.

One day my sister showed me something she discovered, a small box with a sticky black substance inside. She tried warning me, but I was too young and far too foolish to understand. I did not want to believe what she was telling me. I did not want to think that the person who I looked up to with all my heart and soul, might be the one who I should fear of becoming.

There were so many signs. Burned spoons on the balcony, the black marks on her arms, her constant need to sleep. Why would she do that to herself? Why would she have to forget her pain and suffering without trying to deal with it first? Why would she leave my sister and me alone, having to become adults between the ages of eleven and thirteen? I did not know her anymore. I had lost my best friend. She had chosen him over us, engulfing herself into his arms in seek of affection. She scavenged like an animal, searching day and night for her next hit. She was searching for an antidote that would cure the overwhelming sadness haunting her. It freed her from responsibility and motherhood. She did not have to care anymore. She did not have to face the fact that her choices increased the profuseness of her children's agony.

The dark life of opium eaters is a strange and grotesque world. It is filled with demons that still haunt me in the night. Sometimes they visit my dreams and remind me he is still out there, filling peoples' minds with his black magic. His home sits inside of the opium poppy, a flower that is rooted in the deepest, darkest places of the underworld. It sprouts on Earth's surface in the disguise of a beautiful and unique artifact. He targets the most sorrowful souls, replacing emotions with a blank sensation in exchange for their dedication. He is the most venomous snake and does not know when to release his sunken teeth from his weak and cowardly prey. Before I knew it, he was in my life, like a distant relative who would occasionally visit, dressed in my mother's skin. The worst part of all is that she was not his hostage. She was free to go whenever she desired but decided to wear his chains for four long years.

I remember one night my sister and I did not know where our mom was. There was no food in the house, and we did not know what to do for dinner. My sister had twenty dollars, which was a significant amount of money for us at the time. I remember her looking at me as if she had thought of a genius idea, with a smile that seemed to reach out from ear to ear. "You want to order a pizza?" she asked. We shared the rest of the night, laughing and stuffing our mouths. That is one of my greatest memories. It was a time when I was not worried about people's' absences. I enjoyed myself that night. I felt pure joy, just as a normal eleven-year-old should.

These memories seem so long ago, neatly packed away in a box I never wish to open again. If I have learned anything from my experiences, it is that family is more valuable than anything. I would not be the daughter, sister, friend, or student I am today without the constant support I receive from my loved ones. What I know for a fact is without her parents and daughters, my mother would have never attained the success and wisdom she has today. I am glad to say she is the healthiest, smartest, and most beautiful woman she has ever been. She decided to finally put away the chains and focus on what matters in life.

- "The Power of Addiction"- Essay written by author's 15-year-old daughter for her 11th Grade English Class

Hey, I am Aubrey. This is my first year in Youth and Government. Some of you do not know me, then again, a lot of you do, I guess. Let me explain what I mean by that. A lot of you know my name. You know what I look like, who I spend my time with, some of the things I like and dislike. I suppose all of those things are a part of what makes me who I am. But there is something very personal I would like to share here tonight, almost none of you know. It is something that truly shaped me into who I am. Many people try to avoid the word normal. They not only try their best not to fit into the "normal" category, but they would rather be anything but normal. My entire life, growing up, was always so strange and chaotic, that is all I ever really wanted.

Both my parents were addicted to drugs long before my conception. After my mom got pregnant with me, they got their act together, became normal essentially. But as you know, an addiction is an addiction. Long story short, my dad disappeared when I was four years old, and I have not seen or heard from him since. That was thirteen years ago. I heard he is still addicted to drugs and that he got two separate girls pregnant, both of which got abortions.

I always admired my mother for doing the whole single-parent thing until around five years ago when she had a breakdown. Those are the best words I can think of to describe what happened to her. There was a breaking point for her, and things began to go completely downhill for my family and me. My little sister and I watched our mother slowly deteriorate as a human being, after becoming addicted to heroin. During this time, we lived in a house about half the size of this room, and my sister and I slept on the couch while our mom was locked in her bedroom doing God knows what. Either that or she was gone partying, sometimes for days at a time. I took on the role of the parent, not only for my sister but eventually for my mom as well.

After about a year into my mother's addiction, there was an incident at our house, and my grandma came to pick my sister and me up. We thought we were going to stay with my grandparents for a night or two...but it was much longer. It has been four years, and we still live there today. My mom ended up losing the house and everything we owned. She became a homeless, intravenous, heroin addict for about four years, endlessly trying to get sober. For those of you who know me well, you would agree that I am a happy person. I do not seem like someone with such a damaged background. Well, it is the truth, that was my life, and I have emotional scars that will forever affect me.

Today, I am so proud to say that my mom is two years sober and living a normal life. She has a job, a beautiful home, and is such a beautiful spiritual being. My sister and I see her on the weekends and talk to her every day. A lot of you might think it sucks I do not get to see my mom every day, and I am not going to lie, it does suck. But it is better than not talking to her for weeks, or sometimes even months at a time, and not knowing whether she is dead or alive.

My point in giving this speech was to communicate to all of you the idea of strength. I consider myself to be one of the strongest people I know, along with my mom and my sister. I cannot sum up my traumatic experience in a short speech. I could not explain what I have been through, to the full extent, regardless of how much time I had.

However, even after experiencing such a traumatic thing in our lives, my sister and I are still able to be happy. Thanks to our amazing friends and family who supported us and looked out for our best interests, while our mom was struggling to find herself again. We continued to do good in school and be aware of what we needed to be okay. Our mother eventually miraculously overcame her addiction, and we consider ourselves to be extremely fortunate and are beyond happy now.

I do not tell many people this story for fear of them using it to define my family or me. I should never allow anyone to stigmatize or define me or cause dishonor or shame in my life. My life experiences, positive or negative, are a part of who I am and are not what defines me, or my sister, and most of all, they do not define my mother.

Do not ever assume that someone you do not know very well, has not been through a lot, based on outward appearance. Do not assume you know more than others or have experienced more than them. Refrain from treating others badly or unkindly, because, for all you know, you could be contributing to a much larger problem, and they just might break.

My mom always says to tell her story to as many people as possible. She is not ashamed of her addiction because she fought her inner demons and won the battle. She continues her fight against opiate addiction, in hopes she can make a difference in the world, and help others find the joy she now experiences in her life. I asked her if I could talk about this here tonight, and she told me what she always does. She said, "You know Aubs, there are two little girls somewhere in the world, just like you and your sister, who have a mother on heroin. She loves her kids just as much as I love you guys, and they love their mama just as much as you girls love me. Still, their mom is going to die tonight from an overdose because she doesn't have the information to find the help she needs."

I know it sounds harsh. The point is that you never know who needs to have this conversation, or who is searching for help or advice because they are suffering from a condition that you know the solution to. When I was going through that experience, I remember feeling more alone than I have ever felt. I was embarrassed and ashamed of my life. I never talked about it with anyone. So, if anyone ever needs to talk, even if I do not know you, even if it is about something completely different from this, please come to me. I would not want any of you feeling alone, because I know what it is like. I know what it means to feel abandoned, unwanted, and unloved. I also know how it feels when others think you have commitment and trust issues. I DO have those issues, but I continue to work diligently on them every day for the rest of my life!

I want all of you to know that you are loved, you are needed, and you are completely relatable to someone on this Earth if not many. Please do not ever feel alone. I am here for you, as well as everyone in this room here tonight, so please do not ever hesitate to talk to me if you need help with something happening in your life. It does not matter when because I am available for support anytime. Thank you all for welcoming me so kindly. I hope I have a chance to get to know each one of you, at some point during our time here together. Thank you so much for listening.

-This Speech was given by the author's 17-year-old daughter at a "Youth and Government" meeting. A week later, she was voted Statewide Chaplin in her Youth and Government group and asked to give her speech again at a special engagement where she received a standing ovation.

Preface

This book is inspired by my successful recovery from a four-year-long, seemingly hopeless, intravenous heroin addiction. It is my deepest honor and privilege to share relevant information I discovered along the way that continues to fuel my determination to stay clean. I hope a spark will ignite inside your soul, guiding you to the self-discovery of lasting and successful recovery. If you feel like you are sick of your lifestyle and would like to reach a path to enlightenment and freedom, this book will give you the information you need to reach your recovery goals. With the power of your mind, you can break free and achieve the optimal health benefits, blissfulness, and prosperity intended for every person on this planet to enjoy throughout their entire lives.

Successful recovery from Opiate Use Disorder (OUD) is made possible using a specific medically assisted treatment - medication, combined with pure conscious awareness. Opiate Use Disorder is considered a disease because opiates cause isomeric changes in the cells. The drug's analgesic qualities dominate regions of the brain where feelings of pleasure and pain are experienced. Pain is suppressed while pleasure is heightened unmeasurably. When you feel aches and pains or fall sick, these are natural signals from your body letting you know something is not right, enabling you to address the issue and heal from it. Opiates do not cure pain; they temporarily desensitize it while the drug is in your system. Until it is dealt with properly, pain remains dormant in your body, mind, and spirit, causing unhealthy imbalances. These imbalances block your conscious connection to the Universe by limiting your positive thought processes. Mindful medically assisted treatment will show you how you can rebalance your energy centers, reawaken your soul, and find lasting, successful recovery.

I would like to be given the opportunity to share my own personal story of opiate dependence, in hopes that my experiences during my journey resonate with you in some way, igniting that spark, and eventually leading you down the path to happiness and prosperity.

I was born on August 29, 1974, into an average, middle-class suburban household in Van Nuys, California. I was a planned pregnancy and home birth, so my mother had me in the living room of the house that became my permanent residence for the next sixteen years. I came from a tight-knit family, including my two loving parents, who have been married 55 years, and three beautiful sisters, of whom I was the second oldest.

Our parents held a high regard for discipline and respect throughout our upbringing. It was the mid-1970s, and the old "spare the rod spoil the child" prophecy, was a standard disciplinary method for raising children. Advancements in child development, psychology, and sociology had not yet evolved, so many parents believed in corporal punishment as their primary form of discipline. This was "normal" for society back then, while nowadays if you whip your child with a belt, you will probably get charged with child abuse. Regardless, our parents still showered us with loads of love and affection. They did not overcompensate with material possessions, humbling my sisters and me and teaching us to appreciate the beauty of creation and the simpler things in life.

My father had an alcohol problem until I was around thirteen years old. He quit when our family psychologist told him my eating disorder developed because of his drinking. He likely inherited addictive behavior from his mother, who drank and used drugs consistently throughout her life. My mother ran around with him during the sixties, then stopped using all mind-altering substances when she became a Jehovah's Witness, shortly before my conception. My sisters and I were a product of their love, and they always saw our family as their own little tribe. Since I can remember, it was always made clear that we belonged to each other, and nothing could or would ever change that.

I was a shy, above-average little girl during my adolescence, always doing well in school and enjoying activities like reading and writing. I wanted to be a journalist when I grew up, although my mom did not encourage college because of her religion. When I reached my mid-teens, I started developing earlier than my peers, and became insecure about my weight. I remember a boy told me I was chubby one summer, and that was it. I cannot remember if it was because I was overweight, or just because I was starving for attention, but I developed an eating disorder. I went from being an average 100-pound 14-year-old, to an obsessive-compulsive diet freak who looked like a skeleton. It became a serious problem for our family for which we sought professional help. The doctor diagnosed me with Anorexia Nervosa, which I gradually phased out of about a year later.

When I was fifteen, I started rebelling against my parents a little more than the average teenager. I have always had a dominant, opinionated personality, especially during my mid-teens. While most kids this age were rebelling, I was protesting and starting wars. My mom decided my dad should take over with raising me. She felt that he and I shared similar views on life, since she was a devoted Christian, and we were not.

Shortly after my 16th birthday, my father finally gave me the freedom to start dating the guy I had been "in love" with since I was 13. Before we got permission from my dad, it was a nightmare trying to talk, let alone ever see each other. I was climbing out my bedroom window late every night, and jumping back in before my dad got up for work. My parents finally realized that no matter what I was going to claim my independence and were forced to set me free.

As soon as I turned 17, I climbed out of my bedroom window late one night, and ran away to Arizona with my boyfriend. My mother could not offer me the support and encouragement I needed to become a self-sufficient adult, because it was too difficult for her to "let go." I put that in quotations because I know my mama will never let go! She just loves her kids too much. She and I are so much alike in the sense that we want what we want, when we want it. One thing I know for sure is that I would never ask for any other two people on this planet to be my parents. I chose those two wonderful individuals for a reason. From the bottom of my heart, I am sorry mom and dad for any pain I have caused you. You deserve all the best life has to offer and should be proud of what your love created, not terrified and depressed that you might be planning your beloved daughter's funeral soon.

I found out I was pregnant with my first beautiful daughter around six months later. I could say she was an accident, but that would be a complete lie. Her dad and I went to Yosemite on a camping trip one Memorial Day

Weekend with his sister, brother-in-law, and a married couple who were friends of theirs. The couple had the most beautiful little blonde-haired blue-eyed baby boy I have ever seen. I can still to this day remember his name, Kaleb. I had my eye on that little guy all weekend and decided right then and there I wanted one just like that, baby moccasins and all. Nine months later, I gave birth to my own little blue-eyed, tow-headed monster, only I got a beautiful baby girl instead of a boy. I was perfectly fine with that.

Shortly after my 18th birthday, I gave up pretending I was ready to be a mother and wife. My parents tried to intervene and force me to stay with my baby's father, but I was too young and far too unhappy. I knew there was an entire Universe out there to experience and I was in search of something more monumental for my soul. I moved out, got a job as a billing coordinator at a medical office, and soon entered my second love affair – platonic, or so I thought.

He was an ex-Navy Seal who was six years older than me and heavily into drinking and drugs. I had only smoked pot and never experimented with alcohol, making drinking an exciting new venture for me. The next four years were fun, yet both physically and emotionally abusive, carving out the foundation for my intimate relationships over the next fifteen years. Towards the end of our relationship, we started using crystal meth together and I found out he cheated on me with his ex-girlfriend, which also paved out the next decade of my life.

The following six years consisted of me trying to hide my ever-growing fondness for methamphetamines, by living what appeared to be a normal, healthy lifestyle. I had a steady full-time job and made enough money to support my five-year-old daughter on my own, although her dad always helped us financially. I received my GED and was planning to go to community college, majoring in Liberal Arts to become a second-grade teacher. I thought meth gave me more pep in my step, another façade I was conditioned to believe. My boyfriend and I eventually broke up, at which point I entered my next serious relationship without even taking a breath.

I was in my early twenties and deeply involved with a professional drummer who inherited a beautiful home from his grandparents in the hills of Glendale, California. He had the dream of becoming a professional rock star, and devoted years to make that happen. His father studied electrical engineering and wanted all three of his children to get proper college educations. He supported a stay-at-home wife, three children, and managed to save enough money to pay for each of his children to go to any college they wanted, majoring in whatever they felt passionate about. My boyfriend decided on a 4-year master's program majoring in percussion. He received his master's degree when he was twenty-six years old and became a talented and influential drummer.

Shortly after we met, my daughter and I moved into his beautiful home. The beginning of our relationship started off a little shaky because his parents had an issue with the fact that I had an illegitimate child at such a young age. In his attempt to fix things, he decided to propose to me on my twenty-third birthday with a beautiful princess cut engagement ring followed by a birthday/engagement party. He invited all our closest friends to one of our favorite restaurants in Burbank, where his band was performing. It was honestly the proposal I had always dreamed of; the only problem was, in my dreams, it was not with him. He was not my soul mate, and after four years of struggling to make it work, we finally decided to go our separate ways. With no set plans, I packed up my daughter and all our belongings, and moved into my grandparent's house. I lived there contentedly for the next few years, never looking back. I was searching for my soul mate and decided I was not going to waste any more time.

I overheard from a friend of mine, that a peep show theater in North Hollywood was hiring exotic dancers. Stripping had always been a secret fantasy of mine but I never thought I was sexy enough to pull it off. When I went on the interview I was hired on the spot and very quickly started making insane amounts of money. My grandfather was renting the entire upstairs of his house for $600 a month, which was the perfect living space for my little girl and me, so we moved in right away. Six hundred a month was nothing with all the money I was raking in.

I was using meth daily and had recently intensified my habit by advancing from snorting to smoking it. It took six years for someone to talk me into trying it, and that was it, I became instantly addicted. Word got out to my parents that I was using meth, and I decided to take the honest path and confide in my mom about it. She immediately turned on me, becoming completely distant and judgmental. I had reached a low point in my life, and instead of receiving love and support, I was completely shut out of my parents' lives. This forced me to want to use more, numbing myself from the feelings of self-worth permeating through my soul. Meth and alcohol transformed me into a confident woman who did not give a shit what anyone else thought, giving me the courage to speak up for myself and engage in unusual affairs, like stripping.

My mom was deeply negatively influenced by society's stigmatism towards drug addicts. As soon as she discovered someone was using hard drugs, her opinion of them immediately changed, and she would begin judging them in an extremely derogatory way. This is no different than how most people in society are taught to view addicts. Trust me, my mother has come a long way since then.

The 1990's rave scene was in full swing, and I was in my mid-twenties, working as a stripper, making a grip of money, going to raves, and taking ecstasy and meth regularly. Amid all the craziness, I met the love of my life, whose primary source of income came from selling meth. He was a South Korean native who moved to the US with his parents when he was one year old. He barely spoke a word of Korean. He was invited to a party my cousin and I had, and the second I laid eyes on him, I knew he would be the father of my children one day. He was the most adorable, upbeat person I had ever encountered, immediately enrapturing my heart with his positive energy and beautiful smile. I wonder if he still has that beautiful smile of his. I would not know, since we have not seen or spoken to each other in over fourteen years.

We fell into an intense relationship over the next two years revolving around sex and drugs. I was twenty-six years old and felt like I had no real purpose in life. I was tired of our lifestyle and wanted to put it behind us and start a family. He convinced me he wanted the same, but no matter how hard he tried, he just could not put down the meth pipe. I got pregnant with our first beautiful daughter and nine months after giving birth, was pregnant for a third time with another baby girl. I drastically transformed from being a stripper addicted to meth to a wife and stay-at-home mommy. I felt like I had found my calling, doing my absolute best to provide my family with everything I could give them. My children's father found an amazing job due to his past "sales" experience, enabling him to support our family for the next few years.

He never succeeded at conquering his meth addiction, eventually pulling me back down with him when our youngest baby was a year old and I stopped breastfeeding. There was no possible way I could take care of a family with two toddlers 18 months apart. Believe me, I did try, I just could not give them the emotional nurturing they needed while high on meth, making this stage of my life short-lived. Everything started moving very quickly in a negative downward spiral and we both wound up losing our good jobs, our home, and almost our children within a few short months. Without drugs dominating our lives, we really could have had it all. My biggest regret is that we were never willing to say goodbye to our drug-induced lifestyle and focus on our beautiful family.

I willingly admitted to both our parents that I had a drug problem and needed help. After checking myself into a local state-funded rehab facility with our girls, he and I separated for the first time in five years. He decided not to join us, and I lived there alone with our babies for the next six months. During my time in treatment, I found out that my children's father slept with my little sister and one of her close girlfriends. We tried holding on to our relationship for the next couple of years, but anger and resentment made it impossible for us to preserve a healthy bond.

Soon after I left rehab, my little sister died in a freak accident. She was at a party with a group of her close friends and after everyone went to sleep, she and her date stayed up partying on the third floor of the enormous house they were at. According to the guy she was with, early the following afternoon, my sister became aroused because he was ordering them a pizza.

He said she jumped up on the top railing to slide down the rod iron banister, falling backwards 15 feet onto carpet. Afterwards he claims she vomited and collapsed on the floor, and he sat there for over thirty minutes, watching her die instead of seeking help. One of her close friends who was sleeping in the downstairs room must have heard commotion, and woke up to find her unconscious on the first floor. When the paramedics arrived, she was already in a coma and put on life support after shattering her spleen from the fall. When my parents arrived at the hospital minutes later, my dad whispered into her ear, "Rebecca, wake up!" Her heartbeat came back on its own, so the doctors decided to take her into surgery to remove her spleen. About 45 minutes later, my sister and I heard over the intercom, "Code blue in ICU! Code blue in ICU!" We looked at each other in horror. The next thing I knew we were being led into a little waiting room inside the ICU unit. We were all sitting in one chair, piled on top of each other; my dad, my mom, my sister Lisa, me, and Lauren, while a group of about ten doctors worked on saving our baby sister's life. I remember seeing all our other close family members looking through the windows of the double doors crying. The doctors were not able to revive her, and that was it, she was gone.

Her memorial service was the last time I saw my children's father, over fourteen years ago. Shortly following my sister's death, he served a three-year prison term for drug related crimes, and never contacted us again. I raised our two beautiful daughters on my own, until experiencing an emotional break down when they reached their early teens.

My entire life up until that point had been dedicated to making sure my daughters had everything they needed. The absence of their father and my sister's sudden death have always been the core of my heartbreak. This created deep-seated pain and resentment weighing heavily on my soul, and making me feel singled out from the rest of the world. I felt like difficult trials and tribulations only happened to me. I still do not know anyone else experiencing the complete absence of a parent by choice. I was harboring emotional turmoil deep down inside that was becoming too much to handle, pulling me closer to my breaking point. When I thought about it long enough, intense emotions of loss and sadness surrounded me until I could not catch my breath, and would pass out at times.

There was nothing I wanted more than to be the type of role model my precious daughters could look up to and be proud of. I knew deep inside that I could give them everything they deserved but had lost all momentum and focus required to make that happen. I always had a way of justifying things I was doing wrong in my own life by blaming others for my shortcomings. I do not know how I functioned each day and survived with such a negative outlook on life. Destructive past notions that had developed from past negative experiences molded my view of the world, which I noticeably portrayed in every aspect of my life. With chronic depression gaining dominion and lack of emotional support, I lost all strength to pick up and keep moving forward. I eventually gave up and became emotionally absent, and negligent of mine and my children's wellbeing.

Opiates could not have entered my life at a more perfect time. I met a guy who taught me there was a way to temporarily remove built-up pain and resentment, replacing it with pleasure and ecstasy beyond anything imaginable. I watched him enter a painless, divine slumber of blissfulness, and found myself filled with temptation and curiosity of the most volatile nature. I wanted to experience the intense levels of euphoria and ecstasy he was tempting me with. I asked if I could try, forgetting for a moment how scared I was of a hypodermic syringe. No sooner than the words fell from my lips, without any hesitation, he tied a tourniquet around my upper arm and quickly found a vein, pushing the lethal chemical into my bloodstream. And that was it.

The second the dark substance surged through my body, I felt like a caged animal at last being set free into the wild. Now I could live the barbaric existence intended since the beginning of time. Mystical emotions combined with a dark exotic roar rushed through my nervous system, resting comfortably in the untouched, innermost corners of my brain. I had become someone else. I was no longer the sad, overwhelmed, anxious, lonely person I was before. My soul felt like it was wrapped in a soft, warm blanket, embracing me with newfound confidence and security. I possessed a unique feeling of personal power, given the ability to suppress physical, emotional, and psychological pain. I buried deep feelings of guilt and resentment that had been destroying me, and causing such dissatisfaction for so long. I was whisked away to an island where everything was dim, quiet, and far away. A place in my mind where nothing mattered but that very moment. For those first few seconds, I was able to experience heights of bliss I only imagined possible in dreams. The secret, golden mirage hidden deep in the desert of my subconscious mind was a fuzzy, whimsical place. A dreamland from a fairytale. When I did not have access to the drug my existence became so unbearable that being in the fiery pits of hell would be more desirable.

If only I knew then what I know now, I never would have asked for that first hit. After witnessing the negative stigma associated with heroin junkies my entire life, I still lacked knowledgeable information about the danger of opiates. Like what causes opiate addiction? How does it affect the brain and body? Why do people become dependent on heroin? Once you start using, is there a way to stop? I had all these questions and more, that would later be answered through the extensive research I did after choosing to get clean. Had I known more about the daunting effects of heroin addiction I would not have allowed my curiosity to get the best of me. My daughter is right when she says, "opiates seek out the most sorrowful souls."

Using heroin seemed exciting and taboo to me at first. I was completely unaware that over the last few centuries opium has had a powerful grip on mankind, creating more pain and misery than anything in the world. I honestly believed I could easily walk away after trying it once or twice. I cannot find words to describe the feelings that consumed me each time a shot of heroin rushed through my veins. My mind, body, and soul became one with the drug, making it as important an asset as the air filling my lungs. Eventually heroin became all I cared about, and like the millions before me, my soul was swept away by the forceful current of opium. The next four years, I found myself drowning in the deep dark ocean of addiction, with no way out.

The man who put a needle in my arm for the first time left me in the gutter. My children and family rarely spoke to me, knew of my whereabouts, or if I was dead or alive. The only time I was able to see my family was when I was forced to check myself into detox. Otherwise, I was not welcome at my parents' house. They wanted nothing to do with me, and I could not cope with seeing the sadness filling their beautiful eyes the few times I did try to come around. They could not comprehend why I chose a life of misery and debauchery over them. They had every right to feel abandoned and ashamed.

Nobody knew I was suffering from a chronic brain disorder that is easily maintained with proper treatment. The biggest mystery is out of all the detoxes and rehabs I entered, all they offered was methadone maintenance treatment for two weeks. What this means is starting you off on 40 mg of methadone, and each day tapering down your dose. After two weeks, you are thrown back into the world to fend for yourself, and somehow try to stay clean. Drug counselors falsely informed me this is all it would take to eliminate the drug from my body. They also professed that withdrawals typically only last a week or so, with all cravings and severe symptoms expelled by methadone. I suppose that would be true if I continued taking it for the rest of my life. Since this was not the case, two out of the four times I was released from detox, I immediately relapsed, and experienced near-fatal overdoses each time. Frustrated and heartbroken, my family and I continued searching for a solution with no luck.

After my third near-fatal overdose, I felt my time quickly running out. More terrified than ever, I felt death waiting for me around every corner. Essential, lifesaving information every opiate-dependent individual should know about is not commonly addressed in the drug detox and rehab community. I learned the hard way, relapsing and overdosing three times. Hopefully, this book will provide you with protection, preventing you from ever going down the dark road of accidental overdose. I am extremely grateful I was able to live to tell my story, mourning each day for individuals who accidentally took their own life, not being given vital information that could guide them out, before it was too late.

Without success, I continued searching for a miracle that could cure me from this deadly disease. Cursed and alone, I felt like every time I tried to relieve myself of this calamity, I failed miserably. The separation from my children made my opiate addiction grow into a life-sucking monster gaining strength from my misery. The six-times I entered rehab and detox was for all the wrong reasons, so sobriety never lasted more than two weeks. I was only doing it to satisfy my family in exchange for the time spent together in between. The decision was forced upon me in efforts to redeem myself, never genuinely coming from my heart.

After four long years of living this way, all hope was lost in me ever recovering and living a healthy life again. Terrified of getting that call, my family cringed each time the phone rang. Then, on September 25th, 2017, the stroke of a miracle changed everything. I was sick since early that morning, trying to produce enough cash to support my habit. By 10 p.m., I managed to hustle up $500, more than enough to get myself "well." I called my dealer and told him I was on my way to "pick up." He mentioned he had an opiate withdrawal medication for sale and asked if I knew anyone interested. I had never heard of the medication, so I eagerly looked it up online. I rode the Orange Line from Chatsworth to Van Nuys reading all the positive information about the medication. It had a much higher success rate than anything else out there. It said that a person should not start taking it for at least 24 hours since their last dose of opiates, and I had been sick since 7 am. It was now almost 11:30 p.m., which meant that if I played my cards right, in a few more hours, I could start taking the medication without any complications. I figured I had nothing to lose, and the timing seemed right, so I decided to jump on the opportunity. I still could not help but wonder why I had never heard of the medication before.

After exiting the bus, I distinctly remember looking up at the clear autumn night sky. The most beautiful full harvest moon was shining down on me as I took the last walk to my dealer's house. I thought of myself as a small child gazing up at the full moon when I went for rides in the car with my parents. I always felt the moon's energy hovering above, following and protecting me wherever I went. I pictured that adorable little curly-haired five-year-old girl riding in the car with her family, who she loved more than anything else in the world. Everything seemed so much simpler back then. I gently closed my eyes and said to myself, "You've got this girl, you can do this."

Looking back on that night, I had no set plans and had the attitude like, what could it hurt? I tried everything else and thought somehow this would work. When I say I had tried everything else and nothing worked, I am not exaggerating. The truth is, I tried everything presented to me in detox and rehab.

The President of the United States recently announced the opioid crisis a national emergency. This is due to the high number of accidental overdoses happening all over the world. Substance abuse experts have been diligently trying to figure out a solution by making several new OUD medications available to the public. Although most of these medications have proven to be more successful then methadone, it remains the most popular treatment medication used in most state-funded rehab facilities.

After reading the uplifting information online, I decided not to purchase the two grams of black tar heroin I originally came there for. Instead, I bought about a month's worth of Suboxone, which was more expensive than heroin so I nearly spent every dime I had. I was desperately hoping this would be the answer to mine and my family's prayers.

I sent my mom a snapshot of the medication in my hand and called her for the first time in months. She graciously invited me to spend the night at her house, instead of going back to Santa Clarita where I was staying. I missed my girls so much and wanted to see them off to school the next morning and surprise them with the good news. That night was the first time my mom allowed me to set foot on her property in over a year.

Somehow, even though I was in heavy withdrawal, I managed to sleep the entire rest of the night peacefully on my parent's living room couch. I woke up the next morning, with two of the most beautiful little faces I have ever seen staring down at me. My girls. My heart, my life, my soul, my girls. As I saw them off to school, I desperately tried to hide the agonizing withdrawal symptoms I was experiencing. A full 24 hours had passed since my last shot of heroin, and I was feeling it on every level. My mom told me she looked up everything about how to take the medication online, and it said the longer you wait, the better it would work. She continued to coax me into holding off, to ensure everything worked out as planned. I trusted her and held off through the morning, not knowing what to expect after I took my first dose.

After she drove me home, around 1 o'clock that afternoon, I was in so much pain, I could barely find my way up to the apartment. I continued to tell myself, "You can do this! You've suffered through this pain before, just a little bit longer, and this will all be over." I was expecting the worst but hoping for the best. When I could not take it anymore, precisely 36 hours after my last shot of heroin, I placed the medication in my mouth. I was so nervous and distraught; I forgot to put it under my tongue! Shit! Now I was not sure if it would work or not. I thought I would experience instant gratification the moment I consumed it, like when I shot heroin. I did not realize it would take a little while to kick in. I started to panic, thinking for a moment I had spent all my money on another medically assisted treatment failure. I became hysterical, screaming and crying for the next fifteen minutes until suddenly, BAM! It almost felt like a switch went off inside my brain, and I felt normal. What I mean by normal is, I felt like I had never used opiates before in my life. The painful physical, mental, and emotional withdrawals, all my cravings, it all vanished! The difference was as distinct as night and day. I called my family to tell them how I felt. It all seemed too good to be true at first. Over the next few days, I continued taking the same amount of the medication at the same time, and my condition became more and more stable.

I only had enough to last me a month, which meant I would have to find a doctor soon. I found a local Suboxone clinic online and made an appointment for the following day. The second my mom and I entered the doctor's office, the woman behind the front desk told us how fortunate I was to have found help when I did. She said that 70 people had died of fentanyl overdoses in Glendale the night before. She informed us that millions of people were accidentally overdosing on heroin and illegal pills all over the world. She said it was due to fentanyl being added to batches of heroin and pills during manufacturing. Because most people are not aware that it has been added to their illicit drugs, and it is undetectable without special testing kits, people all around the world are self-inflicting accidental overdoses.

That information was terrifying to hear from an addiction specialist, but at the same time made it evident to my mom and I that there was something more to this story. At that very moment I found myself overwhelmed with feelings of gratitude and knew that I had survived three almost fatal overdoses so that I could share my experience to help others before it is too late.

    I have learned so much about what it takes to achieve lasting recovery. I know now that it does not cost thousands of dollars or rob time away from your loved ones. It can be done discreetly, from the comfort of your own home, without missing a day's work. It is inexpensive, and so much easier than you will ever believe possible. The first step is wanting it so bad, you are willing to try anything, in hopes that something will eventually make you better. If you have reached that point, I ask that you please use the information outlined in this book. It was designed to help guide you to your highest goals and true-life purpose here on this gorgeous Earth. Sending out love and encouragement and wishing everyone the best of luck in their journey to recovery.

All my Deepest Love and Support,

R. A.

CHAPTER I

Opium's Origin

"So, stands in the long grass, a love-crazed maid, smiling aghast, while streaming to every wind. Her garish ribbons smeared with dust and rain. Brain-sick visions cheat her tortured mind, and bring false peace, thus lulling grief and pain. Kind dreams oblivious from thy juice proceed thou flimsy, showy, melancholy weed."
—*Anna Seward, 1742-1809*

Each day, more than 115 people in the United States die after overdosing on opiates. The misuse of and addiction to opiates, including prescription, and synthetic forms, such as fentanyl and methadone, is a serious national crisis affecting both public health and social economic welfare. The Center for Disease Control and Prevention estimates the total economic burden of prescription opiate misuse alone in the United States is $78.5 billion a year. This includes the cost of healthcare, lost productivity, addiction treatment, and criminal justice involvement.

Recently, President Trump publicized his concern by announcing the opioid epidemic a National Emergency. A government can declare such a state during a disaster, civil unrest, or armed conflict. Such declarations alert citizens to change their normal behavior and order government agencies to impose an emergency plan.

Statistics show why there would be such a definite need for concern. More than 72,000 Americans died of a drug overdose in 2017, which includes both pharmaceutical and illicit forms of opiates. This is a two-fold increase in one decade. 26 to 36 million people worldwide abuse opiates, according to the National Institute on Drug Abuse. In the United States, an estimated 2.1 million people abuse prescription opiate pain relievers, while over 467,000 Americans are addicted to heroin. These numbers are mere statistics since most people hide the fact, they are abusing opiates, for fear that their families and society will stigmatize them. The opioid crisis happening right now across the world has devastating results for addicts, their communities, and society, as a whole. Government Officials and addiction specialists are in a seemingly endless search of a broad range of solutions to curb opiate dependency and overturn the acute effects of addiction. These statistics are shocking, to say the least; however, the genuine origin of opium is not quite as disturbing.

Opium's mysterious history traces back to a single plant, the opium poppy, also known as *Papaver somniferous*. These beautiful red and white flowers sprout pods filled with a milky white, sappy substance containing the organic pain-relieving alkaloids morphine, codeine, and thebaine. Organically produced, these natural alkaloids have proven to be a blessing for mankind. No other substitute has been found to combat acute, chronic, agonizing pain.

The opium poppy dates as far back as the Neanderthals, who existed between 40,000 and 400,000 years ago and are considered our closest, extinct, human relatives. It is not fully understood what the Neanderthals' use of the poppy plant was, but fossilized seeds have been found in their settlements. This discovery stands as the first evidence of the flower being used by humans.

During the Neolithic period, around 10,000 BC to 4500 BC, also known as The Stone Age, people grew farming crops, which included poppies. Researchers found evidence of the opium poppy in at least 17 Neolithic settlements throughout Europe. They used poppy seeds for baking and oil for cooking and lighting. Anthropologists speculate opium was also used for medicinal purposes and for altering consciousness. The first written evidence of the opium poppy was found in the Nippur clay tablets, written around 7,500 years ago. These tablets are a record of daily life in Nippur, which was the spiritual center of the city-state of Sumer. Sumer is considered the cradle of human civilization because writing was invented there. Sometime around 4000 BC, the Sumerians, who settled in the southernmost region of Mesopotamia, made mention of the poppy plant, which they referred to as *hul gil*, or "the joy plant."

Evidence shows that opium had many uses, in food or as an anesthetic. Opium use has also appeared to have ritual significance. Anthropologists speculate ancient priests used the drug for healing because of its analgesic nature. Thoth, the ancient Egyptian deity, and author of *The Ancient Egyptian Emerald Tablets* takes credit for opium's invention. Isis (goddess of life and magic) gave it to Ra (the Egyptian deity of the sun) to cure a headache.

OPIATE WARRIOR

The opium poppy soon made its way to the Assyrians and Babylonians who extracted the juice by scraping the head of the poppy pod before the flower's blooming. Scraping it this way allowed the sappy white liquid (now referred to as opium latex) to seep out. It was then collected and placed in pots.

Eventually, the practice of poppy cultivation passed onto the Egyptians, who grew vast opium fields in Thebes. In Ancient Egypt, only priests, magicians, and warriors had the privileged right to use opium. Evidence shows that people from Cyprus imported vast amounts of opium in jugs resembling the poppy head. The jugs contained a liquid made from wine or water with opium dissolved in it, which was then used as a sedative. Opium and spices were also mixed and either smoked or drank as an aphrodisiac.

An ancient Egyptian medical document entitled *Ebru's Papyrus*, dating back to 1550 BC, details the many therapeutic uses for poppy seeds. These include calming a crying child, treating breast infections, and reducing pain during surgical procedures. Eye drops and ointments containing opium were also used to treat a broad spectrum of chronic conditions, including asthma and diabetes. *Ebru's Papyrus* contains over 700 known medications containing opium.

Opium cultivation and trade flourished in Egypt under the pharaohs Tutsis IV, Akonting, and King Tutankhamen. This resulted in Phoenicians and Minoans moving to Greece, Carthage, and Europe. The image of the opium poppy frequently appears in Egyptian pictographs, raising the question of whether they used opium recreationally. One example portrays a pharaoh named Homomorphous with wide eyes and dilated pupils, a common symptom of opiate withdrawal. Reports that the pharaoh became weaker and more decayed physically strengthens the theory that he was using. Opium and opium-smoking tools were found in tombs dating back to that period.

By 1100 BC, the cultivation of opium was beginning to appear in Cypress. Growers were using surgical quality knives to score the heads of the poppies, which is still the modern-day method for gathering opium. Egyptians introduced opium to Greece, where they consumed it in a variety of ways, including inhalation, suppositories, and medicinal dressings and bandages. Evidence shows that opium played an essential role in ancient Greek culture. They used a lethal combination of opium and hemlock to put the condemned to death. Many famous paintings created during the 1800s depict Greek deities wearing crowns made from poppy flowers around their heads, flying above Earth, dropping poppy flowers down onto humans.

Ancient Greeks used elaborate mythological stories and deities to describe different issues and problems humans were experiencing in their day-to-day lives. If they were adverse problems, they would personify them with deities from the Underworld. Morpheus, God of Dreams, was one of these such deities. Centuries later, the synthetically modified opiate derivative morphine was named after him.

The story of Morpheus and his family is quite mysterious. Morpheus is a Primeval Greek God. His father is Hypnos, God of Sleep, and his mother is Nyx, Dark Goddess of Night. She births and mothers anything mysterious or unexplainable such as death, disease, dreams, ghosts, witchcraft, and enchantments. Morpheus is the eldest son of Hypnos and the leader of the *Oneiroi*, which in English translates into dreams. He is one of three triplet brothers, who each personify different kinds of dreams humans experience.

Morpheus and his siblings have black wings on their backs, symbolic of the fact that they are gifted with black magic and the power of flight. Morpheus is the leader of the three and has a vital role because he is able to enter the dreams of high-ranking government officials and royalty leaders. Morpheus can mimic any human he chooses by 'morphing' or shapeshifting, thus controlling their subconscious mind during deep sleep. His uncle is Thanatos, God of Death. The entire demonic family resides in The Underworld, in The Land of Dreams. Their kingdom is located beside the River of Forgetfulness and the River of Oblivion. Poppy flowers, and other hallucinogenic plants and flowers, surround their kingdom. Ancient Greeks chose poppies to signify Morpheus because the poppy represents death, eternal sleep, and oblivion. Morpheus himself is said to sleep in a cave filled with poppy seeds.

Around 79 A.D., famous ancient Roman philosopher and author Pliny the Elder described opium's many uses but also warned of its dangers. Around 460 A.D., Hippocrates, also known as the "Father of Medicine," recognized opiate's usefulness as a narcotic and styptic in treating internal diseases and diseases of women. Although he mentioned his concern about excessive alcohol consumption, he never revealed any similar concern toward the use of opium.

Historians are not quite sure how or where China learned about opium, but they think that in 400 A.D., Arab traders introduced opium to China from Thebes. Evidence shows that China has used opium medicinally for thousands of years. Historians are also aware of China's deep understanding of its many uses, and their knowledge of the exact impact it has on the mind, body, and spirit.

During that same year, Hua Tuo, also called the "Chinese Father of Surgery," brewed an anesthetic he called *mafeisan* which translates into "boiled anesthetic." He gave this medication to his patients orally before surgery to make them unconscious. Experts theorize this was a mixture of cannabis and opium since *mafe* is a transcription of an Indo-European word for morphine. Unfortunately, Hua Tuo burned all his recipes before his death, so we will never know what was in his special elixir.

The Golden Age of Islam was from the 7th to the 13th Century. It was an era that honored the arts, science, and culture, all of which flourished under the leading scholars of that time. Medical scholars around this time period, had a serious interest in the development of medicine. Historical evidence shows that many of the uses for opium in ancient Islam are similar to modern-day applications.

Avicenna, also referred to as the Father of Early Modern Medicine, emerged as a great scholar around 1000 AD. In one of his famous books entitled *Canon of Medicine* he describes opium as "the most powerful of stupefacient's." He speaks about its many medicinal benefits, such as an analgesic for gout, sleep aid for insomnia, and a cough suppressant. He also reveals its usefulness to treat diarrhea and as a medication used to sedate excessive sexual desires in men. He noted instances when it should not be used, such as treating gastral intestinal problems like constipation. Opium was applied to patients topically, orally, rectally, and intranasally. Avicenna thought opium should be used as a last resort and preferred to treat the cause of the pain rather than the pain itself. He understood that chronic opium use would affect the proper functioning of memory and reasoning, and that it could cause respiratory suppression, and death.

OPIATE WARRIOR

In 1200 AD, opium had become popular in India. In the late 1200s, during the Mongol Empire, every person from every sector was eating and drinking opium daily. Indian scholars were also contributing their knowledge of opium's medicinal uses to the world.

Then, something odd happened. During the 1300s, opium vanished from history for 200 years. During this time, the Holy Inquisition considered anything coming from the East as linked to the devil. Then out of nowhere it suddenly reappeared in sixteenth century England, in the form of a pill called laudanum. Some people say that an Afghan farmer told opium's mysterious secret to a European settler, and they believe that is how it was originally placed into the wrong hands before spreading throughout the world.

As history reveals, people have been using opium for its many medicinal purposes since the earliest records of human civilization. These ancient societies may have used it medicinally, but never to the extent it is being used today, and rarely was it used recreationally. There is little evidence that the organic alkaloid, pure crude opium, was ever of grave cause for concern. Only if someone used it irresponsibly, which is why recreational use was prohibited. Typically, it was only being used for specific medicinal or spiritual practices. Medical professionals throughout time professed of its excellent medicinal benefits, warning of dangers if used too much. For centuries, humans enjoyed the natural healing elements offered by this beautiful wildflower and opium fulfilled its original purpose: helping people, not hurting them. However, around two hundred years ago, something took a drastic turn for the worse, creating an upsurge in opiate abuse and introducing the first opioid epidemic the world has ever seen.

CHAPTER II

Rise of Western Medicine

"He who for the first time calls upon the opium spirit may see only a beautiful angel with a shining face and hovering wings, but if he would only look behind the apparition, he would see cast upon the background of gloom, a grisly shadow rising vast and awful in the twilight. A terrible warning of judgment and doom. His sorcery has been successful; his incantation has raised the spirit and compelled it to weave its spells around him. But during the short hour of glamour and dream, he has bound himself to the service of a satanic master, whose rule is pitiless and whose reward is death!"
—*Dr. Leslie E. Keeley, The Morphine Habit- from Bondage to Freedom, 1842*

The Industrial Revolution began in England at the beginning of the 18th century. This new era brought exciting advancements in technology, economy, and medicine. People, up until this point, had existed mainly from a homeopathic and agricultural standpoint, relying on their farms and land for survival. As the century progressed, new ideas and inventions were on the rise, transforming energy and turning Great Britain into an industrial and urbanized country.

Agricultural production increased because people were not relying on farm animals to do all the work. New machines heightened the amount of food produced, feeding a larger population, and expanding trade. Hundreds of miles of canals, roads, and railways were designed, new cities appeared, and thousands of factories and mills were built, changing Britain's beautiful landscape forever. This transformation turned Britain into the most wealthy, powerful nation the world had ever seen, ultimately changing our world into what it is today.

There were endless possibilities for a broad range of industries, with new exciting ideas and inventions continuously being born. One of these inventions was going to kick-start the Industrial Revolution: the steam engine, built by James Watts in 1785, used heat more efficiently with less fuel. Coal was crucial during this time because it was used to power the steam engine. This new discovery aided greatly in the production of iron, which in turn was used to improve machines and tools, and build bridges and ships. This strengthened Britain's military power even more.

After coal-fed steam engines were designed, international trade increased dramatically. Coal was then used as fuel for the railways and steamships during the Victorian Era. England had an abundance of coal on its seashores and placed hundreds of coal mines both there and in Scotland. As the Industrial Revolution progressed, and the increasing demand for fuel grew, deep shaft mining soon replaced the old method. This rapidly expanded throughout the 19th and early 20th century, when the industry was at its peak performance.

Following Christopher Columbus and his famous explorations and conquests, Western European powers crushed pre-modern societies and Indian tribes around the globe. Military power was used to subjectify weaker nations with conquest, disease, enslavement, enticement, economic exploitation, forced religious conversion, and ecological devastation of their territories. This social fragmentation became possible by modern advances in science and technology, like the ship's compass, steam engines, heavy gunnery, and the mass production of cheap trade goods. Dominant modern ideologies, brilliantly justified and subdued the entire planet, increasing wealth and power of the civilized nations, and the great corporations of the world. The United States was a young nation, and wars were taking place everywhere. This newly formed era focused its attention on capitalism, industrialism, and science. It was a time when men in the oil and steel industries became wealthy overnight. The rich were placed on a pedestal and grew more productive while the poor were underprivileged and grew poorer, no matter how hard they worked.

As trade expanded, new luxuries and trends quickly developed in Europe. Britain had heard through the grapevine that other faraway lands like India and China had an abundance of unique and exotic items available for trade. A group of British traders decided they wanted to sail to these distant lands, through trade routes Portugal and Spain had already established a century earlier. Queen Elizabeth I jumped on the idea and signed a charter, allowing the men to set sail across the sea to India.

When they arrived, to their dismay, they discovered other European traders had already settled posts along India's shores, so they knew they had competition. After establishing a trading post, barricaded by a large wall, they began devising a plan to abolish the other European traders who had already made their trademark in India. Soon, India realized what a vast commodity their goods were to Britain, and decided to raise their prices, both to the British and to all the other European traders who had been doing business with them for a hundred years or more. As the other Europeans grew increasingly infuriated over the situation, Britain quickly took over, bombing and sinking the other trade ships and blocking them from carrying goods back to their own countries for trade. The European traders created war amongst themselves on the beautiful, peaceful shores of India, which made the Maharaja and his citizens terribly upset.

Try to imagine for a second, exactly what was taking place in India. Let us say you invite a foreign exchange student to stay at your home. While they are visiting, they begin fighting with your neighbors and other members of your household, stealing from you, and selling drugs to everyone in your neighborhood. Now imagine this guest realizes you are in a weak place in your life so they decide to take over the lien on your house and kick you out with nothing. You do not even have enough money to buy food, and you and your family eventually die of starvation. This is what was happening to millions of families in India.

Britain had a ruthless economic agenda when it came to business in India. Some people refer to the seven famines that struck India during the British Raj, from 1770 to 1944, as the worst genocide in human history. The first famine was the deadliest, hitting Bengal in 1770, and killing approximately 10 million people in a three-year time span. It wiped out a third of the population in Bengal and is said to be far worse than the Black Plague that terrorized Europe in the fourteenth century. It was followed by six more severe famines in 1783, 1866, 1873, 1892, 1897, and lastly, from 1943-1944.

After taking over from the Mughal rulers, Britain ordered widespread cash crops to be cultivated, producing export items for high profit. Thus, farmers who were accustomed to growing paddy and vegetables, were now being forced to cultivate indigo, opium poppies, and other items that yielded a high market value for them but could be of no relief to a population starved of food. Eventually Britain drained India of all its most valuable resources and dominated most of the continent. Meanwhile, the East India Company lived in luxury back in England. They built an exclusive British opium refining factory, where starving Indians worked their fingers to the bone hand-packaging each ball of raw opium in leaf wraps and stocking them on the vast shelves of British warehouses prior to export. Ironically, this happens to be the same refining factory which supplies opium for the entire pharmaceutical industry today.

Opium was a huge commodity for Britain because they used it to trade with China for luxury goods like tea, silk, and porcelain. This was ideal because before conquering the major poppy growing regions in India, the British did not have anything China was interested in trading with them. Rather than repress the production of opium, Britain took advantage of another substantial money-making opportunity and began smuggling opium into China through the East India Company. As a result of this trade, opium addiction in China rose steeply. The Qing Dynasty attempted to curb the havoc caused by widespread opium addiction by outlawing its importation and cultivation. In 1811, Joaquin Emperor stated, "This item, opium, spreads the deadly poison. Rascals and bandits indulge in it and cannot do without it even for a second. They do not save their earnings for food and clothes but instead exchange their money for the pleasure of this narcotic. Not only do they willingly bring ruin upon their own lives, but they also persuade friends to follow their example. There is no doubt that opium will harm the morality of our people."

China's attempts to suppress opium use within its borders and British efforts to keep opium trafficking routes open resulted in two armed conflicts. In each of these cases, China lost, and European powers gained commercial privileges and land concessions from them. During the First Opium War (1839-1842), the British government resorted to "gunboat diplomacy" to force the Chinese government to keep the ports in Shanghai, Canton, and elsewhere open to trade. China ended up ceding Hong Kong to the British in the Treaty of Nanking.

During the Second Opium War (1856-1860), the British and French joined forces against China to legalize the opium trade. They also extracted further concessions, including the right to own property from the Chinese emperor's family. In 1858, by the Treaty of Tientsin, opium importation in China was officially legalized. God-fearing British traders claimed the hard-working Chinese were entitled to "a harmless luxury." The opium trade would soon be taken over by less decent hands of desperadoes, pirates, and marauders. Opium began pouring into China in unparalleled amounts and by the end of the nineteenth century, over a quarter of the young adult male population was addicted to opium.

Despite the European success in opening China to trade, many in Europe, China, and elsewhere considered the Opium Wars and the resultant spread of opium addiction to be a villainous and immoral use of military power. In the British Parliament, William Ewart Gladstone denounced the First Opium War as: "A war more unjust in its origin. A war more calculated in its progress to cover this country with permanent disgrace." Gladstone's younger sister Helen suffered from opiate addiction.

In Europe and the United States, it was a time of incredible technological discoveries as well as medical advancements that were about to change history forever. With the massive supply of raw opium being brought in by the East India Company, there was more than enough to go around. Scientists in Germany began testing natural alkaloids and their reactions when mixed with chemicals.

One of these discoveries was made in 1805, by a young up and coming scientist employed with Bayer, by the name of Wilhelm Serturner. He discovered the active ingredient in opium by dissolving it in acid and neutralizing it with ammonia. He named his new crystalline material *morphism*, after Morpheus, God of Dreams. It was another French chemist, Joseph Louis Gay-Lussac, who introduced Serturner's substance under the name morphine to the world. Gay-Lussac was a professor at the prestigious *Ecole Polytechnique* and had the academics and social credentials that Serturner lacked. With Gay-Lussac's support, morphine was available throughout Europe by 1822.

Morphine was considered a huge medical breakthrough because physicians who had been working with raw opium had to deal with natural variations in potency. Depending on the batch, a specific dose might have little effect or be lethally strong. With morphine, it was easy for doctors to standardize dosages, and because morphine was much stronger than raw opium, far less was required.

Critics spoke negatively about the drug, due to the high number of suicides and murders resulting from its use. In Balzac's 1830 presentation of *Comedy Du Diablo*, the devil credits morphine with a sudden population increase in hell. After becoming addicted to morphine, himself, Serturner commented on it, saying, "I consider it my duty to attract attention to the terrible effects of this new substance so that calamity may be averted."

In 1874, C. Alder Wright, an English lecturer in chemistry and physics, and researcher at St. Mary's Hospital Medical School in London, England, made another medical discovery. He found that by diluting morphine with acetyl, in a pot on his stove, he could produce a highly potent substance without the common adverse morphine side effects. It was not until after he died in 1898 that another young chemist, also employed with Bayer, by the name of Heinrich Dreser, continued to test the new compound. He worked with Bayer to begin the massive production of diacetylmorphine, which quickly got coined the name heroin, because it made people who it was tested on feel heroic.

Scientists and doctors believed that because they had separated the active ingredient from raw opium, it would somehow be safer to use. Heroin was marketed as a non-addictive pain medication as well as a morphine substitute and cough suppressant. Bayer also promoted heroin for the use in children suffering from coughs and colds. A 1900 catalog for Dow's Anti-Trust Drug Store in Cincinnati, Ohio, glamorized heroin as "the safe substitute for the opiates." They also claimed that "it acts as a general analgesic without narcotic influence."

By 1899 Bayer started producing an abundance of heroin, exporting it to twenty-three different countries. Heroin became available as pastilles, cough lozenges, tablets, water-soluble salts, and an elixir with a glycerin solution. Heroin was the main ingredient in many patent medicines that were easily accessible at most over the counter pharmacies throughout the United States and Europe. Before anyone saw it coming, the first United States opioid epidemic came to fruition.

You might wonder where German pharmaceutical companies were obtaining the acetyl. Before the invention of gasoline, where were these petrochemicals being produced? When most people think of Bayer, they immediately think of aspirin, but this is just one of the thousands of medicines manufactured by IG Farben using oil derived compounds.

At the turn of the century, a young man by the name of John D. Rockefeller Jr. had become extremely wealthy from striking oil. He quickly rose to power, dominating 90% of the oil refineries in the United States. Rockefeller, unsatisfied with his multibillion-dollar production of oil, searched for a way to use coal tar, a petroleum derivative, to manufacture plant-based synthetic substances as medicines. His idea was inspired decades earlier by his father, Bill "Devil" Rockefeller Sr., who sold bottles of raw petroleum mixed with opium as a cure for cancer. Rockefeller Jr. just needed a vehicle to extend on and capitalize petroleum derivatives as medicines.

He began his mission by purchasing shares in what was to become the largest and most powerful chemical and pharmaceutical cartel the world has ever seen. IG Farben partnered with several other massive German chemical manufacturers including Bayer, Hoechst, and BASF. This conglomerate would later invent, produce, and distribute the Zyklon B poisonous gas that was used to kill over 200 million innocent people in Nazi concentration camps during World War II. IG Farben initially built Auschwitz as the largest industrial complex in Europe before transforming it into a human extermination camp. Executives employed with IG Farben were among those found guilty of war crimes and sentenced after the war ended. In 1939, I.G. Farben purchased $20 million worth of high-grade aviation gasoline directly from Standard Oil of New Jersey, owned by Rockefeller. That same year a "Drug Trust" alliance was formed between Standard Oil and the German pharmaceutical company, with the Rockefeller empire taking 15% of the stock. After World War Two, IG Farben was dismantled but later emerged as separate corporations within the alliance. Well- known companies included General Mills, Kellogg, Nestle, Bristol-Myers Squibb, Procter and Gamble, Roche, and Hoechst.

From the late 1800's and well into the 20th century, opium addiction skyrocketed across the U.S. while John D. Rockefeller was trying to establish a new scientific approach to medicine. His biggest obstacle was figuring out a way to take natural homeopathic herbs and remedies people had become accustomed to for centuries and wipe them out of existence. People would then be forced to rely on synthetically produced medicine as a primary form of treatment. It did not take long for John D. to devise a plan to patent plant-derived semi-synthetic medications that German scientists at IG Farben synthesized for him. If an organic compound like opium is mixed with synthetic chemicals it becomes patentable. In ensuring that all their medications treated the symptoms instead of curing diseases, they likewise ensured that illnesses would last longer, making profits higher. This would especially be true if the person were to become dependent on the drug for the rest of their life.

The American Medical Association was formed in 1847 with the stated aim of enhancing the medical profession's position in society. It was a small, weak organization until John D. Rockefeller and Andrew Carnegie took on a "philanthropic mission" aimed at helping the AMA gain power. The medical profession supported scientific medicine because it met the economic and social needs of physicians. With support coming from all sides, "Western medicine" was established as the traditional form of medical practice in the United States.

John D. Rockefeller and Andrew Carnegie were two of the wealthiest people in the world. Together, they strategized a plan to put an end to all forms of holistic or homeopathic medicine, demoralizing and discrediting its practitioners and consolidating the power of so-called "modern medicine" for the next hundred years. This "new and improved" industrial approach to health, prioritizing profits over people, would play a part in the downfall of the very country that gave birth to it. Kind of sounds like the plot to a bad movie, right? Unfortunately for anyone in America it is a daily reality.

In 1910, the oligarch and the steel tycoon hired a well-known American educator by the name of Abraham Flexner to write a detailed report, publish it, and submit it to Congress. The report concluded that there were too many doctors and medical schools in the United States and suggested that all-natural healing methodologies, which existed for thousands of years, should be labeled as "unscientific quackery." From this point on, "quackery" became their code word for "competition".

Flexner's report called for the standardization of medical education. From then on only allopathic AMA (American Medical Association) institutions would be granted medical school licenses. Congress acted on the conclusions and made them law. Society is conditioned to believe that the AMA looks out for patients who are taking prescriptions to ensure their safety, when in reality, their job is to make sure no homeopathic, natural remedies hit the surface, and people find out how to really cure diseases.

There were many types of doctors and natural healing modalities that soon became Rockefeller's biggest competition. He wanted to eliminate these competitors, thus ensuring that drugs would be the main form of treatment. Capitalists like Rockefeller and Carnegie embraced scientific medicine as an ideological weapon in their struggle to formulate a new culture appropriate to and supportive of Industrial Capitalism. They used their tax-exempt foundations to offer massive grants to medical schools that would only teach an allopathic curriculum. Curricula in the schools were dismantled, removing herbs, plants, and the importance of a healthy diet from standardized lessons and causing this ancient knowledge to slowly fade from public consciousness over the following decades.

Scientific medicine was named for the fact that it replaced healing as art and represented a method of practice that was based on verifiable facts instead of dogma. As the Industrial Revolution rose to its peak, population levels exploded; this new form of medicine treated disease as an engineering problem rather than a human health condition, and this approach was naturally suited for handling far greater numbers of patients than doctors had traditionally been expected to treat.

This also had the effect of making doctors more dependent on capital-intensive therapies, especially pharmaceuticals. Patients, lacking firsthand knowledge of herbal remedies, would now have to go through a physician to obtain the benefits of modern-day medical research. Although this gave doctors more control, it came with a hefty price, as they became one of the many scapegoats blamed for the wide spread of opiate addiction due to their overprescribing of patients – a practice heavily encouraged by the pharmaceutical companies.

With the American Medical Association and allopathic medical schools firmly in place, the abolition of other natural medicines, and the enforcement of regulated licensing of doctors, Western Medicine continued to expand and gather more wealth and power. The pharmaceutical empire that Rockefeller built also includes vaccines, sedatives, analgesics, antibiotics, heart drugs, and hypnotics. The Rockefeller Foundation donated over $32 million to medical universities that would teach and indoctrinate the names and uses of thousands of synthetically produced drugs.

The American Medical Association's primary objective is to discredit and eliminate anyone who might pose a potential threat to the success of the rise of Western Medicine. Included was any college or university across the U.S. that did not want to participate in changing to the new teaching modalities. Those schools would be shut down and quickly replaced by new ones that went along with teaching medical science. The new curriculum trained doctors to be drug peddlers for the biggest, most powerful drug cartel in the World, IG Farben. It is interesting to note that the words pharmacy and pharmaceutical are derived from the Greek word "pharmacia," which means "potion, witchcraft, sorcery, or to administer poison."

From 1861 to 1865, during the American Civil War, thousands of injured men were treated with morphine. After putting their lives on the line in one of the bloodiest wars in history, they became scapegoats blamed for widespread opiate abuse in the United States. After the war ended, it was said that these men brought their opium habits home with them, thus influencing the rise of morphine and heroin addiction. Morphine and heroin were no longer referred to as "God's own medicine"; due to the rise in addicts, it was now looked down upon, soon coming to be known as "the army drug."

In 1906, the American Medical Association approved heroin for medical use, with the understanding that it was powerfully habit-forming. Although people were aware of the addictive properties in heroin, it had little effect on the patenting of its use in medicines. Bayer owned the patent for heroin, but it was not difficult for local pharmacists to make it themselves and add it to their own personal miracle concoctions. This came to an end in 1906 when the patent medicine industry was exposed, and Congress passed the Pure Food and Drug Act. This forced pharmaceutical companies to list all the ingredients on their products.

After that seemed to have zero effect on the consumption of heroin recreationally, the Harrison Narcotics Act of 1914 was passed, making the non-medical use of narcotics illegal. By then it was too late, as the high demand for heroin had already set a long supply chain into motion. An underground market had formed to meet the needs of the millions of addicts who were created after a decade of heroin's glamorization. Negative stigmatism towards heroin addicts gradually evolved, conditioning society to support dogmatic principals. When heroin addicts were not stealing to support their habit, they were collecting scrap metal to sell, thus creating the negative reference, "junkie."

As World War II began, trade routes between Europe, Persia, India, and Turkey became blocked. With all the injured soldiers, morphine was in high demand. Since access to opium was slim to none, German scientists fell into a bit of a problem. They worked overtime to mass produce a synthetic substitute and in 1939, scientists at IG Farben synthesized a compound labeled as VA10820. They developed so many different synthetic compounds that year, it was not until 1942 that they were finally able to test it as a painkiller. Several experimental trials were performed on VA10820 without good results. Researchers underestimated its strength, and the doses were too high, resulting in unbearable side effects. For these reasons, the medication was never brought into widespread usage in the Third Reich.

It was not until after the Vietnam War ended in the 1960s that the medication was introduced to heroin addicts in the form of methadone maintenance. It was estimated that many Vietnam veterans would return home heroin addicts, a problem that was already flourishing across New York City. Methadone, being a full opioid agonist, has the same influence over the brain and body as heroin and morphine. It is designed to stay in the system longer, sometimes as much as 24 hours, which is why it was chosen as an opiate withdrawal medication. The truth is, a person taking methadone is still fully addicted to opiates, it just comes in a different form and lasts longer. The only reason withdrawal symptoms subside is because methadone is being substituted for the illicit drug instead. Methadone does not make cravings go away; it merely satisfies your craving for your opiate drug of choice. As soon as people stop taking methadone, they start experiencing withdrawal symptoms ten times worse than those caused by other full opioid agonists, giving most people no other choice than to relapse.

OPIATE WARRIOR

Fentanyl is a modern-day synthetically-produced opioid and is the number one cause of overdose deaths in the world. It is highly lethal, inexpensive, and can easily be purchased from China on the internet. The most frightening thing of all is that, as with opiates of any kind, there is no quality control involved. Wherever refining takes place, fentanyl can be added to a batch without a person having any clue. Therefore, many underground pill laboratories have recently been responsible for tens of thousands of overdose deaths around the world. These illegal black market labs ordered fentanyl online and used it as the main ingredient in their illicit pills.

The most common forms of heroin currently on the market are "black tar" heroin and "China white" powder. Black tar heroin is typically dark orange, brown, or black, and can be sticky and tar like, or a hard rock that resembles coal. It is the most common form used in the western hemisphere of the United States since the mid-1990s and is usually smuggled across the Mexican border. China white powder typically dominates the eastern half of the United States, and does not actually come from China, but gets imported into the United States from Columbia.

The process of refining heroin and then smuggling it into the U.S. is not an easy task. Despite border patrols and vice operations trying to stop the smuggling process, heroin still gets carried across the border daily. Smuggling heroin is a pervasive process and drug lords, involved in the refining process, usually hire "mules" to transport the drugs over the border safely. These people are paid thousands of dollars to hide the illegal substances in different parts of their bodies. Typically, they will swallow large amounts of heroin in condoms, and then excrete them once they arrive safely at the desired location. After heroin is refined from the original opium poppy flower, it will go through a long process of hiding, smuggling, cutting, and passing through dozens of hands before reaching the buyer. At that point, extraordinarily little of it is pure.

Opium became a downfall for humanity the moment it started being used recreationally, without heeding the warnings of our ancestors. A drug so powerful that it can completely take dominion over a person's life, regardless of who they are or where they come from. When used to satisfy selfish desires, opium becomes all a person can think about and eventually their life will revolve around it, beginning a downward spiral leading to misery, incarceration, and death. The first opioid epidemic started a little over 200 years ago, meaning that for thousands of years ancient civilizations kept the use of opium under control. Although so many people in society used opium, historical reports of addiction and overdose deaths are slim to none.

It is unfortunate that not everyone could carry the due diligence our forebears seem to have possessed. They understood opium was a unique and sacred gift from the gods. For centuries, men and women wrote of its many benefits and dangers. It was made clear that consuming too much, or using it for the wrong purpose, could be extremely dangerous and possibly lethal. If ancient civilizations could have kept this sacred secret out of the hands of the wrong people, opium might have remained a beautiful and beneficial resource for humans. Instead, a hunger for greed and power transformed something so bright and promising, into the darkest, evil, most deadly epidemic, humanity has ever had to face.

CHAPTER III

Addiction's Creation Story

"Addiction is a terrible thing. It can wipe down entire cities with just a single taste. It can destroy relationships, break up families, and reveal undiscovered worlds."
—Kylie Grace Dae Kim, Power of Addiction Essay

A ddiction has been plaguing humans since the turn of the century. This toxic condition impacts billions of people worldwide, but somewhat surprisingly is a reasonably modern phenomenon. It was created in the 19th century by medical and moralistic interest groups who drastically altered its original context for their own selfish endeavors. Until then, the actual word had a completely different meaning.

The word "addict" draws its original meaning from an ancient Roman myth that tells the story of a slave named Addictus. Emancipated by his master, he chose to wander the land in his chains despite having the freedom to remove them. It makes sense that the modern-day meaning derived from this myth; the dependent person appears to be enslaved, carrying addiction's heavy chains while possessing the free will to remove them whenever they choose to.

Shakespeare was the first well-known writer to use the word addiction in its original context in one of his plays - *The Life of King Henry V,* written around 1599. In a tense moment near the start of the play, the Archbishop of Canterbury describes Henry V as a great sovereign and intellectual, adding that this is "a wonder" because as a younger man:

"...his addiction was too courses vain,

His companies unlettered, rude, and shallow.

His hours filled up with riots, banquets, sports.

And never noted in him any study,

Any retirement, and sequestration,

From open haunts and popularity."

As the play unfolds, Henry V's youthful preference for raucous socializing to the detriment of his kingly studies becomes known to his archenemy, the Dauphin of France. The Dauphin becomes overconfident, as England's friends and enemies alike speculate on how the King's youthful addiction could be affecting England's military strength, but all come to find King Henry proves invincible in battle and magnanimous in victory. The King's addiction becomes forgotten in the final act of the play, but the concept remains with us to this day.

Traditional English usage of the word was well established long before it appeared as a formal definition in the first version of the Oxford English Dictionary, published in 1884. This definition reappeared virtually unchanged in all subsequent editions until 2010. The wording has been brought up to date but the essence of the original meaning was preserved.

Here is the definition as it appears in the 2010 edition of the Oxford English Dictionary: "The state or condition of being dedicated or devoted to a thing, esp. an activity or occupation, adherence or attachment, esp. of an immoderate or compulsive kind."

Many modern-day great thinkers referred to addiction in a variety of ways. Plato, in *Republic*, referred to habits as "master passions." He believed that they could play a central role, in the political degeneration of democratic city-states into murderous tyrannies. He spoke mostly about addictions to power, sex, raucous revelry, and violence. He never mentioned drugs, although drunkenness is mentioned amongst the addictive possibilities.

Eight centuries after Plato, in his work entitled, *Confessions*, St. Augustine poignantly discussed his struggles to overcome his two most overwhelming addictions: to romantic love, and to social status. He wrote about battles against addictions of all sorts in the late Roman Empire, which he described as a kind of enslavement. Not suffering from this enslavement of the soul was an essential part of the Christian path to happiness.

Seventeen centuries after St. Augustine, Sigmund Freud abandoned his medical view of addiction and alcoholism as symptoms of psychological disease rooted in the brain and unconscious life of individuals. In a flash of insight, late in his life, he characterized addiction and many other psychological problems as the inevitable product of modern industrialized civilization. In his book, *Civilization, and It's Discontents*, he suggests that modern culture must be put to the analyst's couch, for addiction to be controlled.

Many other contemporary thinkers developed similar ideas about the relationship between addiction and the structure of society. In *Confessions of an English Opium-Eater*, written in 1821 by Thomas De Quincy, the author describes his addiction to opium plainly and bluntly. When the piece became published in London Magazine, the public did not react to the news with shock or judgement. Instead, the piece received exhilarated recognition and great reviews. It was accepted in England during that time for people of all social statuses to use opium daily; they were referred to as "opium eaters," consuming the drug orally in the form of a pill called laudanum. A negative stigma towards opiate-addicted individuals was not common until after the Industrial Revolution. As soon as modern Capitalism began dominating most of the world, the word addiction suddenly changed its meaning from an adjective into a verb.

Before addiction was addressed as a human health condition, it was of little concern to anyone. This deadly disease did not exist as we know it today until after morphine, heroin, alcohol, and millions of pharmaceuticals were produced to enhance the effects of natural alkaloids. The meaning went from being a somewhat silly metaphorical way of describing someone's heightened interest in a specific habit, to being the name of a very harmful brain condition. This was after opium and other natural alkaloids began to be synthesized in a lab, making them much more potent and easier to produce, and therefore able to affect more people. When the hypodermic needle was invented and pressed into use shortly afterwards, opiate users could now inject these powerful new substances directly into their bloodstream, bringing reliance and addiction suddenly within reach for all.

Wikipedia offers only the modern-day definition, whereas the original meaning has been long forgotten in most of today's literature. According to Wikipedia, addiction is defined as:

"A brain disorder characterized by compulsive engagement in rewarding stimuli despite adverse consequences."

This new meaning fits in perfectly with a strategy to make people believe they are powerless over an incurable disease, and can only hope to maintain their condition through constant treatment. This typically involves prescription drugs or state-funded detoxes and rehabs which support this neo-capitalist agenda. The original word and its meaning were lighthearted, meant to describe an innocent habit or attraction to something. It did not carry any medical or scientific meaning. The modern-day definition of addiction identifies itself as a deadly global epidemic that creates misery and death for those taken captive by it.

In order to ever abolish this disease successfully, it is fundamentally important that the negative stigma associated with people suffering from opiate use disorder be put to rest. Until the victims are viewed from a more positive perspective, without any judgement or criticism, opiate addiction will continue growing in pandemic proportions. Fearful negative thoughts and emotions bring about a mirrored outcome. This disconnects you from your true nature which only recognizes emotions associated with love, forgiveness, acceptance, and gratitude. The stigma associated with opiate dependence is simply a constructed web of mental conditioning that has been entangling society's perspective on many levels for an exceptionally long time. This illusion forces everyone to believe they are powerless, not only over addiction, but over a wide range of other habits as well. As

Deepak Chopra says in The Secret of Healing – Meditations for Transformation and Higher Consciousness- "just as the silkworm spins its cocoon and is caught in it, so do humans weave the web of their own concepts and are caught in them."

For decades, Alcoholics Anonymous has been teaching its members that in order for you to become "sober," you must first admit you are powerless over drugs and alcohol, surrendering yourself to a higher power in order to be set free. What they fail to mention is that YOU are your higher power. Transforming your thoughts is the key to experiencing freedom. Fear and doubt will continue pulling you in a downward spiral, until it eventually takes your life. That is the inevitable truth behind opiate addiction - most people do not survive.

Being caught in the middle of the web of lies and deception barricades you from any hope or beacon of light. Transforming your future into one surrounded by love and acceptance will produce a positive transformation, fueling your determination to get clean. The time has come for you to be part of the greater good of mankind by ending the vicious cycle of addiction in your own life and then helping others to find enlightenment. Remember, humans survived happily for thousands of years in a world where addiction, as we know it today, was nonexistent.

A window of possibility will begin to open, creating a conscious shift in your awareness. The more this information is spread, the faster everyone will begin to clearly see the hidden truth behind the history of opiate addiction, putting an end to this miserable madness before it completely takes over and dominates the human race forever.

CHAPTER IV

Opiated Opioids

"People who use heroin in this society are not particularly vulnerable to fear of what might happen to them. They are frightened and depressed about what has already happened to them, although they may not be fully conscious of that fact. The sources of real joy in their lives become so diminished that the superficial pleasures of heroin and other drugs loom large by comparison. Even before they touch heroin for the first time, these people are profoundly suffering. What they need is joy in the fullest sense of the word. They already know quite enough about pain."
—*Deepak Chopra. Overcoming Addictions, the Spiritual Solution*

Before anyone goes on a crusade to stop addiction, it is beneficial to have a clear understanding of opiates and their influence over the central nervous system. Most humans love to experience pleasure but cannot bear the thought of enduring any kind of pain. This includes physical, psychological, and emotional trauma-based pain, built up from childhood into adult life. To acquire a full understanding about the cause and effects of opiate addiction, the meanings of certain unfamiliar terms related to OUD recovery and treatment is essential. Frequently these terms are phrased in

a medical context, making them confusing and inaccessible to many, but again – understanding is essential, and worth the effort in your battle.

Opioids are synthetically produced drugs like heroin, morphine, oxycodone, and fentanyl. Opiates are natural alkaloids, like opium itself. The thing opiates and opioids have in common is that they all bind to opioid receptors located in the brain, spinal cord, and gastrointestinal tract of the human body. Some opioids are endogenous, meaning they are produced naturally in the body. One example is endogenous morphine, more commonly known as endorphins. This is a chemical your brain releases when you experience intense levels of pain. Other opioids are considered exogenous, meaning they come from the environment, like morphine, heroin, and fentanyl. These types of opioids are produced synthetically in a lab. The actual plant derivative opium, however, is considered an opiate, because it is produced organically and grown from the Earth.

To better understand how opioids work, let us imagine a region in the brain tissue where opioid receptors are present. In the absence of endorphins, inhibitory neurons secrete a neurotransmitter. This prevents nearby neurons from releasing the chemical dopamine. Exercise and sex cause the release of this same chemical which then activates the three primary opioid receptors located on the inhibitory neurons. These receptors are the Mu, Delta, and Kappa receptors, and are also responsible for controlling a person's mood, behavior, decision making, and consciousness. As endorphins bind to these receptors, the inhibitory neurons are blocked from releasing dopamine. This allows the dopamine secreting neurons to unload dopamine freely. The dopamine then gets picked up by a third neuron in the same area. When dopamine release takes place in pain-processing regions of the brain, the result is feeling less pain. When dopamine is released in the reward pathways of the brain, the result is a calming effect that feels good.

The purpose of the reward pathway is to train the brain to repeat activities that will cause dopamine-mediated pleasure. When opioids stimulate this reward pathway, the brain learns to want to repeat only that behavior. Dopamine can help with pain control as well as induce an incredible state of euphoria and pleasure. In strength, this far surpasses anything naturally occurring in the regions of the brain controlling the reward pathway, creating an emotional high.

There are several routes a person can take to allow the drug to reach the brain. The slowest method is eating it in a pill form. Another standard practice is burning black tar heroin, China white powder, or crushed pills on a strip of aluminum foil and inhaling the smoke. This method is commonly referred to as "chasing the dragon." People enjoy doing it this way because the drug enters the bloodstream through the lungs more quickly. Smoking opium and heroin usually creates a more difficult withdrawal, since the chemicals are absorbed into the lungs and held longer in the body. The third, and quickest way for the drug to reach the brain is through intravenous injection. People use pills, heroin, China white powder, and a variety of other substances this way by mixing them with water, and then "cooking" them on a spoon, or with a "cooker." A tiny ball of cotton is then placed in the cooker, at which time they draw the liquid up, through a hypodermic syringe, find a vein, and "shoot" the substance into their body. When the drug is done this way, the substance immediately enters the bloodstream, having a massive effect on the user. Typically, the faster the exogenous opioid reaches the brain, the stronger the relationship between behavior and reward, making it nearly impossible to discontinue use once someone starts doing it this way.

The difference between natural opiates and synthetically made ones is that the more opiates are refined, the more the chemical structure changes, and the stronger they become. Higher potency means a greater dopamine release. The chemical composition in all exogenous opioids mimics erogenous opioids. Pleasure and reward are heightened, forcing the user to want more. Once the reward system becomes familiar with these heightened levels of dopamine, this becomes all it wants, and physical, emotional, and psychological dependence quickly take dominion over the mind and body. Other man-made substances that mimic natural opioids and release higher levels of dopamine are alcohol, cocaine, and methamphetamines.

For decades, specialists have been trying to figure out why addiction is such a significant problem for millions of people around the world, while others seem to be untouched by it. In the early 1970s, drug professionals believed that the great appetite for morphine, heroin, and cocaine caused permanent cravings in all mammals, including humans. Addiction specialists performed some slightly sadistic experiments using laboratory rats housed in metal cages with drugged water. They were trying to prove that if taken long enough, anyone, no matter who they were or where they came from, would become addicted to drugs like heroin and cocaine. They believed it was the chemical hooks in these substances that turned people into drug-crazed fiends who would stop at nothing until they got their next "fix." This myth was the backbone of mainstream addiction theory during that time.

To prove this hypothesis, scientists took a lab rat, and put it by itself in a metal "Skinner Box", with two water bottles. One water bottle was filled with regular water, and the other was filled with water laced with either cocaine or morphine. The rat would almost always prefer the drugged water and usually killed itself from a self-inflicted overdose rather quickly. It was all over the news how "Skinner Box" rats consumed vast amounts of heroin and other addictive drugs. They were sometimes so absorbed in dosing themselves, they would forget to eat, and die of starvation. In those days, this got interpreted as scientific proof that drugs like heroin were so irresistible that a person, like any other mammal, would become lost forever after experimenting with them only once.

In 1971, Bruce T. Alexander was given a job at a local Vancouver city drug rehab, to counsel and oversee citizens addicted to heroin and methadone. His career goal was to attempt to help addicts stop using both. He was also a professor of psychology at the local university. Dr. Alexander noticed that in the "Skinner Box" experiment, they were putting rats in an empty cage, with nothing to do but drink the drugged water. He decided on an experiment to prove that these addiction specialists were basing their conclusions on dogmatic principals and influencing society to go along with their false beliefs. He referred to their theory as the "Demon Drug Myth" or the "Old Story" about addiction.

In his experiment, which he called "Rat Park," he took several rats, both male and female, and created what some would refer to as a utopia for rats. The rats had anything they could need or want to be satisfied and live happy, fulfilled lives. They had toys, tons of food, other rats to play and mate with, and were basically living a rat's dream. They also had the two water bottles, one laced with heroin, and the other filled with regular water. The only difference was, in this cage, the rats rarely ever drank the drugged water, none of them ever drank it consistently, and none of them ever overdosed. You went from 100 percent overdose when they were alone and isolated, to zero incidence when they had active and connected lives.

The Rat Park experiment influenced other addiction specialists to research further, conducting thousands of tests on a wide range of people for over a decade. They concluded that the majority of individuals, using the so-called "addictive drugs," in reasonably healthy social environments, did not become addicted. Dr. Alexander and his little group of researchers were hoping their studies would rid the world of the "Demon Drug Myth" forever. Unfortunately, it did not work out this way.

Nonetheless, Dr. Alexander went on for many years studying the causes and effects of opiate addiction in the lives of individuals, their families, and society as a whole. Through his extensive studies and over 30 years of addiction expertise, he concluded that there are several other well-documented risk factors that increase the likelihood of addiction. These include things like degrading poverty, early-life traumas, family dysfunction, depression, loneliness, racial prejudice, insidious advertising, perfectionism, predisposing genes, deliberately addicting social media, games, and insidiously designed gambling machines. He believed that the structure of modern society tilts the playing field in favor of addiction by increasing the likelihood that people become exposed to most of these risk factors, and many others, as the consequence of social and economic forces beyond their control. Modern society also tilts the playing field by making it difficult, for people who have acquired harmfully addictive lifestyles, to find deeply satisfying alternative ways to live.

Addiction specialists from the distant past had a much deeper understanding of the causes of opiate addiction and how to properly treat it. If their extensive research were taken seriously and indoctrinated into modern-day addiction treatment, we would not be in the desperate situation we find ourselves in now. Dogmatic principals continue to have a strong influence over society more than 30 years later, costing millions their lives. Opening our hearts and minds to anyone who has fallen victim to the opiate habit will allow them to find the help and support they so desperately need. The cause of the problem must be addressed and done away with before we will begin to notice any kind of change. Heart-felt love and acceptance are vital if progress is to be made, allowing people a chance at peace and survival.

The importance of Dr. Alexander's experiment should not be lost on someone struggling with opiate dependence. It is easy to view addiction as a personal failure, and too often our family, friends, and pop culture will echo that sentiment, leaving one feeling as though this whole mess is one's own fault. While it is important to take personal responsibility for the choices that led you to this point, it is also important to realize that we do not live in a perfect world, and the need to escape the pain and frustration of reality is proven to exist in more mammals than just humans – in other words, your escape is a natural response! But that does not mean it is a healthy response. Understanding the difference is an important step in choosing a better path.

CHAPTER V

Love is not Tough

"When love and spirit are brought together, their power can accomplish anything. Then love, power, and spirit are one."

—*Dr. Deepak Chopra*

Many social, environmental, psychological, and genetic factors determine whether a person will develop a drug or alcohol dependency. Addiction does not discriminate against anyone, so unlike most social groups and religions, it accepts you regardless of who you are or where you come from. Members are not chosen based on sex, age, race, or religion. Anyone willing is welcome, and addiction does not seek out individuals suffering from trauma because sooner than later, they will find it on their own.

Prized members are the lonely, sad, broken, and beaten down, who are so isolated and distanced from normal society that they desperately search for anything worth bonding with to help them cope with the physical, psychological, or emotional pain they are experiencing. The more traumatized or depressed a person is, the higher their chances are of developing an addiction. This can be to organic interests like sex, eating, and exercise, or it can be to something unnatural and severe, such as drugs and alcohol.

Many theories and conclusions have been drawn by addiction specialists over the years. We witness them in a seemingly never-ending search for answers as to what causes addiction, and what the most effective methods for treating it could be. Throughout the ages, they have produced several different theories, none of which have been greatly beneficial. This is proven by the high number of accidental overdose deaths still happening all over the world, with numbers rising by the second. In full support of the Capitalist agenda, a negative stigma began to develop towards individuals suffering from drug and alcohol dependency. Society started questioning whether addiction was a choice or a disease, giving rise to a heavy debate. For many years, this topic has carried a dark cloud; a stigma which surrounds the lives of anyone touched by addiction. As a result, addicts are typically shamed, judged, criticized, and looked down upon as weak and irresponsible.

During the latter half of the 20th century a method for treating addicts developed, one which was essentially an authoritarian form of confrontational counseling. Addiction counselors saw clients as out of touch with reality, dishonest, incapable of responsible self-direction, deficient in knowledge and insight, and pathologically defended against change. They saw their role as one to help correct error, combat delusion, take charge, educate, break down the addict's defenses, and become the client's link to reality. The task was one of installing supposedly 'missing pieces', often involving the client paying large sums of money to begin the process.

In the late 1940s and early 1950s, such treatment centers were a successful business venture, giving rise to an approach to the treatment of chemical dependency that was widely replicated in the following decades. The first stage of this approach was the emergence of the concept of "tough love". This method of treatment instructed parents and loved ones of the addicted individual not to enable them in any way, which many times got misconstrued. This concept became widely popular, teaching that the more you push the addict away, the more complicated their life will become, speeding their descent towards "rock bottom", at which point – in theory – they would begin taking accountability for their actions and seek sobriety.

In 1973, Reverend Vern Johnson proposed the use of a technique of "family intervention", a method through which the bottom became raised to meet the addict. In this exercise, loved ones staged a professionally facilitated confrontational meeting with the addicted individual to share detailed feedback on the person's drug use and how it affected them personally. Then they would request that the individual take specific actions to resolve his or her drug problem. This usually involved offering an ultimatum that if they did not choose to seek treatment, the support of the family would be cut off and they would be left to fend for themselves.

Three propositions emerged about family adaptation to drug addiction:
1. Addiction is a family disease.
2. The homeostasis of the addict's family gets maintained through elaborate defense mechanisms of all family members. For example,

denial portrayed metaphorically as the elephant in the living room that no one acknowledges.

3. Family members inadvertently support the continued course of addiction through their enabling (e.g., excuse making, overcompensating, rescuing, or helping in any way that involves drug use).

In other words, the early model of addiction as a disorder of an individual was stretched to include family members and significant others. This depicted them as being pathological in defending and enabling the addict, generally unconsciously. Loved ones were instructed and encouraged to practice "tough love", a concept established on four interrelated theories:

1. Addiction is rooted in an immature, defective character encased within an armor-plated defense structure.

2. The seemingly passive methods of traditional psychotherapies are hopelessly ineffective in penetrating this defensive structure and altering deformity of character.

3. The addict can therefore be reached only by a "dynamic change" that breaks through this protective shield.

4. Verbal confrontation is the most effective means of engaging and changing addictive behavior.

As addiction treatment was being established in the U.S. and other First World countries, one of its main goals was working on trying to separate what a man is from what he seems to be, states himself to be, or would have us believe he is. It was postulated that people with alcohol and drug use disorders possessed a characteristic pathological personality structure - basically, their immaturity and egocentricity were making them incapable of perceiving reality. The addictive personality was alleged to include a cluster of ingrained defense mechanisms, such as denial, rationalization, and outright dishonesty. Aggressive high-volume confrontation was believed to be the only way to break down the addict's formidable wall of defenses.

How well did these confrontational forms of treatment work? A couple of years ago, a father admitted his 19-year-old daughter into a local drug rehab for heroin addiction. He stated that his son was accepted to seven Florida drug programs between the ages of 18 and 23. The most prolonged period of sobriety his son was able to attain was 11 months. His father stated, regarding why he thinks his son lost his life, that "My son became plagued; he wanted to stop, he asked for help repeatedly, and in the face of all the professionals, we continued to attempt to help. Finally, we gave in to the professionals. We decided that "tough love" was the answer, and we would no longer accept our son's phone calls, refused to provide financial support, and let him hit rock bottom. The professionals told us this was the only way, and we listened. The result for us was that our son died of an overdose in a McDonald's bathroom, alone."

The mirror opposite of authoritarian confrontation is the empathic, client-centered way of counseling introduced by psychologist Carl Rogers in 1980. He believed it was the counselor's role to hear and understand the client's dilemma and evoke their motivation for change. Rogers trusted in the natural desire for people to grow in a positive direction when given the proper conditions and motivation. When people feel unacceptable as they are, they are immobilized and unable to change. Experiences of shame, guilt, and humiliation typically favor the status quo. Indeed, if suffering cured addiction, there would not be any. What people need instead is to experience understanding and acceptance, enabling them to see themselves as they are. In experiencing understanding and acceptance, people are then free to change. To test his theory, Rogers carefully defined three conditions he believed a counselor should provide to foster positive change: empathy, honesty, and acceptance.

During a study conducted in the United States in 2016, it became relevant that most heroin addicts were severely depressed over situations in their immediate family environment. In cases where one's parents were divorced, estranged, or otherwise absent, many continued using opiates to cope with the emotional pain they were experiencing. They chose to medically numb themselves, separating them even further from their loved ones, causing more pain, and creating a vicious, never-ending cycle.

To be successful at recovery, you must acquire a reliable support system from family and loved ones. Love, encouragement, and a stress-free environment are vital if recovery is to be successful. Most people suffering from Opiate Use Disorder who relapse after completing treatment lack the support they so desperately need from their loved ones. For this reason, they face the possibility of accidental overdose and death.

Family members have a difficult time showing people suffering from Opiate Use Disorder the love, encouragement, and support they need to stay clean. This comes from the negative social conditioning that is directly associated with opiate addiction. The process of "tough love" has led to millions of overdose deaths all over the world, happening at astounding rates. To live in love, we need to release our emotional pain, negative conditioning, and anything else that, like a cloud, obscures our true, radiant, loving nature.

When you were first born, you needed love to survive, and that has not changed. From the beginning of life as we know it, humans were given the glorious gift of love, which is the essential key to unlocking a happy, fulfilling life. Many people are unable to recognize the vital role love plays in allowing humans to enjoy healthy, long-lasting lives. Love is not the opposite of hate; being whole, love has no opposites. Some claim fear as its opposite, while others believe it to be disconnection. When your life becomes absent of love, both of these negative qualities exist. Love is as equally precious and life-sustaining as the air you breathe. Without it, everything becomes dark and distorted, and life seems to have no real purpose. Humans are created to experience love and fulfillment throughout their entire lives. Lack of love is responsible for much of the calamity and suffering we see in the world today.

Thousands of years ago, the Bible described love this way: "Love is patient and kind. Love is not jealous. It does not brag, does not get puffed up, does not behave indecently, does not look for its own interests, does not become provoked. It does not keep account of the injury. It does not rejoice with unrighteousness but rejoices with the truth. It bears all things, believes all things, hopes all things, endures all things. Love never fails." – 1 Corinthians 13: 4

With the power of love, anything is possible. Love is the impulsive evolution that expands life, dancing in the freshness of the unknown. It has been described as one of the most intense emotions we experience as humans. Love is a variety of different feelings, states, and attitudes, ranging from interpersonal affection to pleasure. It is an emotion you feel deep within your soul that carries with it no limits or conditions for a person. A passion you feel for another, so pure and sacred, nobody can genuinely define it to its true extent. Love is what a person feels for another without any physical or mental barrier between them. When true love is present, you live purely to be with one another, sharing and accepting any experiences, pleasures, problems, or pain that comes your way. Regardless of the circumstances, it does not matter, you still love and accept each other no matter what. Love is the act of caring and giving to someone despite any consequences, and having another person's best interests and well-being as a priority in your life. This kind of love is regarded as unconditional affection and carries no limits or conditions. Unconditional love means that you guard each other with your life and would do anything for one another, and no betrayal or abandonment could ever harm you. When you love someone, you want nothing more than for them to be genuinely happy, no matter what it takes, allowing their needs to come before your own. You hide nothing of yourself and can tell them anything, because you know they accept and love you just the way you are, including all your faults.

Ancient Greeks believed in four types of love: Eros, Phileo, Storge, and Agape. Eros love is used to describe a romantic kind of love, a love felt deep in the body, one that causes trembling, excitement, happiness, and joy. This type of attachment gives a person butterflies in their stomach when they think about the other person. Eros is a state of the heart, intimately related to sex but more expansive – Eros love can lead to sex, but it also leads to children, family, joy, and laughter.

Phileo love is where you give to receive, making it easy to express love and affection. It is regarded as the love of the soul, or "brotherly love." It embodies cultures and beliefs. It is the connection you feel towards people who have similar interests, social graces, and styles. It can also be the kind of love God has for us, Jesus had for his disciples, and a parent has toward their child when they are proud of them. Phileo is soul love, and its strength and power will depend on the height of the bearer's soul.

Storge is the love of community and family. It is often dutiful, sometimes unfeeling, but nonetheless, extremely powerful. It is a natural love, but strong enough to be a hindrance to spiritual growth, especially when family and culture are holding you down. It is a love that may pull you towards a lesser path like the love one feels for opiates. This type of love can be so powerful, it blinds you from the fact that opiates are not the cause of joy and pleasure in your life, but creating more pain for you and your loved ones than you are consciously aware of.

Agape is more of a parental, mature, sacrificial type of love. *Thayer's Greek-English Lexicon* beautifully describes Agape love as such: "To take pleasure in a thing, prize it above all other things, be unwilling to abandon it or do without it." Agape is a form of strong love you feel for another individual making it difficult to let go. Agape love is usually at a cost to the bearer. It puts the beloved first and sacrifices pride, self-interest, and possessions for the other person's sake. Agape is the kind of love we are commanded to have for one another. It is considered a love of supreme greatness. Loving someone in this way can often involve loving so much, you put their needs ahead of your own, even if sometimes it hurts. Agape love is what parents should exercise towards their addicted child if they want to witness positive change and growth. By demonstrating Agape love towards someone with a drug or alcohol dependency, they will no longer feel pressured or forced to change. Agape love will open up an area for positive growth to come about effortlessly on its own.

Exercising tough love towards your addicted loved one and shutting them out of your life when they have nothing else to live for will cause them not to care if they live or die. All they want is to be accepted. Imagine how you would feel if your parents completely shut you out of their lives when you needed them most. Imagine having a terrifying, life-threatening disease and feeling alone and lost in this big dark world. A person suffering from opiate addiction who is not receiving the proper support and encouragement from their loved ones, will feel like the only thing worth living for is the freedom from pain provided by the drug. The core reason for their addiction is the pain and suffering they feel inside created by past negative conditioning. Experiencing more pain and misery will only cause them to intoxicate more, until they eventually become lost forever.

Tough and love do not even go in the same category in the first place. Tough is something rigid and hard, whereas love is the most beautiful expression of affection you can offer another person. Until it becomes clear to society that the old way of dealing with opiate addiction is only making matters worse, and the healers refocus their attention towards the cause of addiction, overdose deaths will continue to haunt us. Agape love will show someone that they have everything to live for, fueling their desire to get clean on their own.

I would like to end this chapter with a quote from one of my favorite people in the world, who helped me so much in my search for a lasting solution. Dr. Deepak Chopra, in his book *The Seven Spiritual Laws of Success,* put it very simply by saying: "Practicing the Law of Giving is very simple: if you want joy, give joy to others, if you want love, learn to give love, if you want attention and appreciation, learn to give attention and appreciation; if you want material affluence, help others to become materially affluent. The easiest way to get what you want is to help others get what they want."

All you really need is to feel loved and accepted. Your brain operates on a reward system, and love is a reward that creates feelings of joy and appreciation for everyone involved. Any love, acceptance, and gratitude offered to someone suffering from drug dependency will be returned to you when they successfully conquer their inner demons. You will quickly notice a change in their attitude and determination to get clean. The more positivity and encouragement you shower them with, the more you will receive back because what goes around comes around. Love, forgiveness, support, and acceptance are expressions that will bring the addicted individual back from the dark place they are so desperately trying to escape. Judgment, criticism, stigmatism, isolation, and worthlessness create a vicious cycle, forcing the addict to numb their pain with opiates, inevitably making death their only way out.

CHAPTER VI

Mindful Medicine

"When you walk across the fields, with your mind pure and holy, then from all the stones, and all growing things and all animals, the sparks of their soul come out and cling to you, and then they are purified, and become a holy fire in you."

-An Ancient Hasidic Saying

A piece of legislation making its way through Harrisburg is looking to regulate prescriptions of Suboxone, one of the most successful medications used to help combat opiate addiction. Sponsors of the bill say that the drug has recently been abused. Senator Michelle Brooks claims that this bill would prevent the abuse of the addiction treatment drug by requiring office-based prescribers to be licensed, while at the same time pairing the drug with addiction counseling. Also known as buprenorphine and naloxone, Suboxone is currently prescribed by health care practitioners who have a license through the federal government with no oversight from the state. This new bill would license office-based prescribers of Suboxone, impose a fee for licensing, and allow the Department of Drug and Alcohol Programs to provide oversight and licensure programs.

State health officials say this would create unnecessary barriers for people trying to stay clean off opiates. They feel it would limit what they have been actively trying to do, which is to expand the number of physicians working to receive their federal waiver for buprenorphine, and increase access to the medication. If this bill gets passed, it will require prescribers to pay an annual licensing fee, which might stop them from trying to get licensed to prescribe the medication. Opponents of the bill say this would decrease access to the drug, which in turn would increase overdoses.

The federal government ultimately oversees all medically assisted treatment in the United States. Prescribers of these medications must pay a yearly tax to treat patients. The government places limitations on how many patients a given prescriber can treat per year, as well as strict rules and regulations they must follow. Broken regulations are punished by loss of license, meaning they cannot prescribe the medication to opiate addicts anymore. They are trying to claim it is because people have been abusing it, but people abuse other opiate prescriptions, like painkillers, just as readily. Aren't people addicted to prescribed opiates and overdosing and dying from them? Where are the restrictions for overprescribing those kinds of medications? If anything, it should be the exact opposite. Opiate prescriptions should be monitored and restricted, while the medication used to help people should become available to everyone who needs it.

The government has been negotiating medically assisted treatment regimens since the very first opioid epidemic in the 1800s. The first known successful form of medically assisted treatment that helped people suffering from opiate addiction came from a Civil War surgeon by the name of Leslie Keeley. He developed a phenomenally successful (yet controversial) method of assisting people suffering from the alcohol, tobacco, and opium habits. He called his approach the Double Chloride of Gold Cure, and it was said to have helped close to a million addicted individuals during his 30 years of operation. Although his method is referred to as "quackery" (aka competition), the statistics do not lie. He never revealed the exact ingredients in his cure, and the information supposedly "went with him when he died," so nobody knows the correct method he was using. This was during the same time John D. Rockefeller and Andrew Carnegie were developing a way to discredit herbal and homeopathic medicine. Dr. Keeley's Gold Cure was discredited, as were many others, although it showed promising signs for improvement in drug addiction therapy.

In the 20 years that Dr. Keeley dedicated to the study of people who had fallen victim to the "opium habit," he developed a hypothesis of how he believed opiate addiction affects a person psychologically. He found that, the psychological action of opium was to diminish the natural forces of the nervous system. It arrests the legitimate processes of nature and prevents the nerve fibers from fulfilling their accustomed duties. When the drug gets used for a long period, it produces an isomeric change in the nerve fiber which results from the continued and excessive use of various drugs such as bromine, chloral, tobacco, alcohol, ether, opium, and morphine. He believed that the molecule of opium may hold a relation as close to those of the nerve in this pathology as are the molecules of hydrogen and oxygen in water. A physical union takes place between them and modification of movement of the molecules of the nerve that is the basis of the opium habit. The victim's nervous system has an added factor in its structure as well as function, and a victim is a man or woman plus opium or morphine. The individual is as much under its control as any other function of the nervous system. They have no power over the drug and their addiction becomes a dominant force in their life. Dr. Keeley concludes his study by saying, "It is the general testimony of confirmed opium eaters that the will power is lost; they are mere machines carrying out the behest of an imperious master, and their own volition is no longer a factor in this case. Morphism is that condition which results from the process of isomeric change, in which the functions of the nerves, the liver, spleen, kidneys, stomach, and other organs become robbed of their natural powers, their energies get curtailed, and the entire system is subject to the falsifying influences of a destroying drug."

A variety of assisted treatment medications have received approval from the American Medical Association and been put on the market. However, to this day, the most popular treatment medication in most state funded rehabs remains methadone maintenance. Methadone was synthesized in Germany in the laboratories of IG Farben in 1939. IG Farben is also the pharmaceutical company that invented morphine and heroin. Methadone is a full opioid agonist, having the same effects on the brain and body that morphine and heroin have; the only difference is you are no longer using illicit drugs.

Methadone is administered at clinics and hospitals under the direct supervision of a doctor or medical staff. This is a strict requirement because if the drug is misused, accidental overdose is very likely. Methadone has the same effects on the central nervous system as heroin and pharmaceutical opiates. Your cravings do not go away, you merely begin to crave Methadone instead. It is just as addictive and even more difficult to detox from, because it stays in your system longer than any other opioid.

Scientists at Bayer and IG Farben initially synthesized methadone as a substitute pain medication for morphine to help injured soldiers during World War II. Many reports stated that the drug was not widely used due to dangerous side effects like nausea and the aforementioned tendency for overdoses. Some people who the drug was tested on showed signs of euphoria, inflammation of the skin, toxicity, and an appearance of illness, and rapidly developed a tolerance to it. Methadone had a high potential to be addictive and create other health problems as well. Despite these claims, the manufacturer's advertisements stated that the drug had "little risk for addiction."

When World War II ended, German patents and other assets got distributed to the allies. IG Farben's developments were confiscated by the U.S. Department of Commerce Intelligence division. They were brought to the U.S., and by 1947, methadone was approved as a painkiller. It became widely used in this country, and gradually people started to become addicted to it. By 1955, there were 21 methadone addicts reported in the UK. By 1960 there were 60 known addicts, and the numbers continued to rise.

Researchers at the Rockefeller Foundation started distributing Methadone in doses to help people suffering from opiate withdrawal, even though most people relapsed as soon as the withdrawals subsided. It was proposed to the administrators of New York City, where approximately half the country's addicts lived, that methadone clinics be established. This was to treat heroin addicts and get them off the illicit drug. From then, methadone treatment for heroin addiction spread across the U.S. and into adjoining countries.

By 1998, there were 44,000 people on Methadone maintenance in New York State alone, and 79,000 across the world. Since Methadone is a long-lasting drug, it could be used as a treatment method. Most patients on Methadone maintenance can get through an entire day without feeling any withdrawal symptoms. Methadone was helping some people maintain stability, while other people chose to use the drug illicitly and abuse it. The number of people dying due to their illicit use of Methadone started to increase at alarming levels. The number of people who died from Methadone overdoses in 2001 equaled the number of Methadone overdose deaths from 1990-1999. At the same time, deaths from other opiates were increasing at a similar rate.

Some drug specialists argue that using this form of medically-assisted treatment is merely substituting one drug for another. The only kind of opiate addiction treatment that fits this description is Methadone maintenance. Most patients require 80-120 mg of Methadone or more to achieve the proper effects, and require treatment for an indefinite amount of time. Given in such high doses, patients typically report feelings of euphoria and sedation. Like most prescribed medications, methadone is considered a corrective but not a curative treatment for opiate addiction. Lower doses may not be as effective or provide the blockade effect.

People experiencing withdrawal symptoms from Methadone describe it as the most horrifically painful thing they have ever experienced. It seeps into your bone marrow, staying in your system longer, and creating a longer withdrawal time. Typically, Methadone maintenance treatment becomes an endless endeavor due to the severity of withdrawal symptoms.

The most successful medication used in the treatment of Opiate Use Disorder is Buprenorphine and Naloxone. Buprenorphine is a partial opioid agonist, meaning it works partially like other opiates, only with a much weaker effect than full agonists like heroin and Methadone. A beneficial quality of Buprenorphine is that it was developed with a ceiling effect, so the effects level off even with further dose increases. This lowers the risk of misuse, dependency, side effects, and accidental overdose. The second half of the medication is Naloxone, known as an opioid antagonist or blocker, was initially added to the mixture so that if intravenous drug users tried to inject it, they would immediately go into severe withdrawals. It blocks the effects of euphoria from the Buprenorphine, while at the same time blocking any cravings, thoughts, or urges to use opiates. It is the same medicinal compound used in Narcan; a medication distributed to people after they suffer from an overdose. The blocking effect immediately stops the effects of the opioid, and the person will usually snap out of it. Combined, these compounds transform into a miracle medication, allowing you to clear your mind and focus on rebuilding your life again.

This combination of medication comes in two forms. Suboxone, which is an orange-flavored strip, and Zubsolv, a little mint tablet. They are both sublingual which means they are placed under the tongue or inside the cheek until they dissolve. They come in several different strengths so that when the time comes, your doctor can taper down your intake until you no longer need the medication. Most people continue taking Buprenorphine and Naloxone for at least a year, depending on their level of dependency to opiates. Common withdrawal symptoms and cravings for opioids like heroin and prescription pain medications is completely diminished.

Before taking this medication, it is fundamentally important for you to know that you must wait at least 24 hours since you last put opiates in your body. Doing this will bring you maximum benefits and success in this difficult struggle for freedom. Not taking it properly in the beginning will make you assume it is not working, and you will begin to experience more severe withdrawal symptoms than you started with. The key to taking this medication correctly is waiting as long as you possibly can since your last dose of opiates. People who have tried going this route and complain that it does not work for them probably did not wait the required amount of time necessary.

Obstacles have been designed for those trying to get prescribed Suboxone and Zubsolv. The fact that it was not synthesized in the lab of IG Farben might be the reason. Buprenorphine was discovered in 1966, at a home products company called Reckitt and Colman who knew that opioids with structures substantially more complex than morphine could selectively retain the desirable actions while shedding the undesirable side effects. Their main goal was to find such an opioid. They had two failed attempts before finally putting Suboxone into clinical studies. When it was first presented at medical conferences, pharmacologists were attracted to the fact that it was an effective pain killer without high potential for abuse. The potential of it being used as a drug treatment for narcotic addiction was also recognized. Despite this realization, it took almost three decades before it was used therapeutically. Over forty years later, Suboxone is now considered to be the gold standard of medically assisted treatment.

Zubsolv has comparable efficiency and safety, as well as the same active components as Suboxone. The broad choice of six different strengths offers the potential for finer tapering and individualized dosing with potentially fewer tablets compared to existing substitution treatments.

In July 2013, Zubsolv was approved for the maintenance treatment of opioid dependence by the US Food and Drug Administration (FDA). In August 2015, the product also received approval for induction treatment of the same patient population. In November 2017, the EU Commission approved Zubsolv for the treatment of opioid dependence in Europe, and at the beginning of 2019, it was also recommended in Australia.

A longitudinal study was conducted in 2016 to test the overall efficiency of Zubsolv. The review was a success, with 978 of the 1,080 patients confirmed as being evaluable for treatment. From the patients evaluable for treatment, 77.6 percent were determined to have been a treatment success, defined as a patient who completed 28 days of treatment and tested negative for opiates on the last follow-up drug screen.

Obstacles might make it challenging to obtain a prescription for Suboxone or Zubsolv. The medication is expensive, so not having private insurance will require you to spend approximately $1800 or more from your own pocket at the pharmacy each month. Having proper insurance coverage will require you to only have to pay for your doctors' visit and a small fee for your script. This amount can range anywhere from $100 to $500.

After you pay the fee and your doctor hands you your prescription, it can be filled at most local pharmacies. Suboxone and Zubsolv are uncommon medications in some places, so it might have to be ordered and, depending on the availability, picked up later. If you plan it right, you can start Mindful

Medically Assisted Treatment the second you have the medication in your hand. To achieve best results, detox on a water fast while waiting for your prescription to come in. As soon as you pick it up from the pharmacy, take your first dose. The longer you wait, the better it will work, improving your chances at successful and lasting recovery.

To find a doctor in your area, go online and search for Suboxone or Zubsolv doctors. After entering your zip-code, several prescribers in your vicinity will be shown. Try contacting as many local doctors as you can, asking them how much they charge for the first visit and prescription fee. You will probably be able to find one that is not as expensive as the rest. Regardless of how much they charge, if you have insurance to cover the cost of the medication, it will cost far less than heroin or pills. I found a doctor in my area who charged $100 to write the script. Since I have Medi-Cal, when I went to the pharmacy and picked up my prescription, I did not have to pay anything. If you search hard, you should be able to find something similar. Depending on how bad you want this, seeing that you have taken the first step on your own, the Universe will handle everything else.

It takes roughly around 15 to 20 minutes for this type of medication to reach your brain through your bloodstream. Do not panic, just relax, because even though you are probably experiencing the height of your withdrawals and you are scared it will not work, I promise it will work better than you can possibly imagine. You will feel like a switch went off in your head once it reaches your brain, forcing your withdrawals and cravings to completely vanish and making you feel like you have never used opiates before in your life. Continue taking the same amount at approximately the same time each day and watch your life unfold into endless possibilities. Stay on the medication for as long as you need to. When you feel you are ready to stop, you and your doctor will discuss a tapering schedule and the same tools outlined in this book will be used. Taking Buprenorphine and Naloxone will not get you high. It will only enable you to restore the mental clarity which is the very first step in setting yourself free from the bondage of opiate dependency. Express gratitude for the massive leap you just took towards achieving lasting recovery! I am extremely proud of you for staying so strong! I knew you could do it!

CHAPTER VII

Returning to Consciousness

"If you are quiet enough you will hear the flow of the Universe. You will feel its rhythm. Go with this flow. Happiness lies ahead. Meditation is key."
—*Buddha*

Ayurvedic medicine is a 5,000-year-old science which teaches us that balance is our true nature, a fact easily witnessed through the observation of every organ and cell in the human body operating in balanced tandem. In Sanskrit, "Ayurvedic" means "the knowledge of life and longevity." Your body naturally informs you if something is not right, so problems can be addressed and you can heal from them. Your personal connection to the Universe is made possible by energy flowing from various energy centers located throughout your body. This allows your soul to connect with Divine energy frequencies emitting from the Universe. When this energy fluctuation becomes disrupted or blocked, it is impossible for you to reach higher levels of consciousness. Blockages are repaired using certain techniques that allow you to enjoy the good health, success, and prosperity intended for every human on this planet.

Your brain is constantly sending out ultra-sensitive electrical currents, giving you the instinctual feeling of wanting to set goals and obtain higher levels of progress and achievement. Thoughts pour out in the form of electromagnetic energy waves, dictating which path you choose to take. Your natural state of consciousness will lead you to enlightenment, freedom, ultimate success, and total well-being, since this is your true nature. Negative past experiences from childhood and into your adult life condition your thought process, causing you to make unwise choices and pulling you further away from achieving any positive goals. Pondering on contrary, unfulfilling goals, desires, and needs creates negative energy. The Universe gathers negative energy and returns it back to you in the same form, resulting in undesirable experiences. If your thoughts are aimed towards positive goals, desires, and aspirations, then this is what you will receive back. The Law of Attraction and Quantum Physics are based on the concept that your thoughts and emotions create your reality. Everyone on this planet holds the power within their minds to create whatever kind of life they want. When you are operating on the level of pure conscious awareness, you open the door to endless possibilities for total wellbeing, happiness, fulfillment, lasting prosperity, and infinite abundance, which is essentially your birthright.

At the time of birth, and throughout the first few years of life, you are aware to some extent that you are completely loved and completely lovable. This sense of security becomes lost somewhere along the way from experiences that leave a lasting negative effect on you. Negative conditioning comes in many forms and from several outlets. The most common types of conditioning come from your parents, siblings, friends, school, work, and the media. Mental conditioning is created by anything or anyone you come into direct contact with throughout your life that influences your perception of the world around you. You begin feeling like you are not good enough, or unworthy of happiness. Negative mental conditioning should never be blamed on another person. We are all doing our absolute best with what we were taught from someone close to us that we trusted.

The media constantly influences thoughts and emotions, making you believe you must look a certain way or have material possessions and affluence to be accepted in society. If you do not fit into a specific category, you end up feeling like you are not capable of living a happy and fulfilled life. By the time you are five years old you begin to pass judgement on yourself and others. Everything you see and hear up until that point molds you into what type of adult you are going to be. Criticism and judgement take over as you begin to develop an ego. This ego is not real, but merely a false construct, designed by society, to build a gap between you and your conscious connection to the Universe, thus separating you from your innate ability to create the life of your dreams.

Addiction is another cause of disconnection from your conscious reality. A person in the modern era can develop an addiction to a variety of different habits like food, sex, porn, exercise, television, shopping, and work. Truly, many of these habits are pushed on us daily, even glorified, until people become so used to them that they are overlooked and seen as harmless. However, they are still just as habitually excessive, affecting the central nervous system in the same exact way, causing your brain to release higher levels of dopamine. So, you are not the only person who has an addiction problem. Many people become habitually addicted to situations that do not seem to pose any threat to society.

Depressants like alcohol, opiates, opioids, and several other mind-altering substances exert their effects through different areas of the brain. The main one is the proper functioning of GABA, short for Gabapentin, a chemical which regulates mood and anxiety in the brain. Mind-altering substances modify electrical signaling inside the body. Opiates of any kind cause you to become "dissociative", meaning you no longer feel any connection to your environment or the people around you. This occurs when signals are blocked to the conscious mind from other parts of the brain.

Working as a centrally active KOR agonist, opiates directly influence the claustrum, which is the region of the brain in which the KOR becomes most densely expressed. When functioning normally, this area of the brain dictates behavior, decision making, and conscious awareness. It is theorized, based on its structure and connectivity, that claustrum has a role in coordinating a set of diverse brain functions, the most crucial one being consciousness. Lesions of the claustrum in humans is associated with disruption of consciousness and cognition. Electrical stimulation of the area between the insula and the claustrum produces an immediate loss of consciousness, and recovery of consciousness occurs upon cessation of the stimulus. One theory suggests that claustrum harmonizes and coordinates activity in different areas of the cortex, leading to the seamlessly integrated nature of subjective conscious experience.

What exactly is consciousness, and why is it so crucial for human existence? Modern research has defined consciousness as: "Any experience, cognition, feeling, or perception." The dictionary's definition of consciousness is: "Sentience or awareness of internal and external existence." Meanings of the word consciousness extend throughout several centuries, which include many associated related purposes.

One formal definition given in Webster's Third New International Dictionary states consciousness as being:

1. Awareness or perception of an inward psychological or spiritual fact: intuitively perceived knowledge of something in one's inner self.

2. Inward awareness of an external object, state, or fact.

3. The state or activity that is characterized by sensation, emotion, volition, or thought: mind in the broadest possible sense: something in nature that gets distinguished from the physical.

4. The totality in the psychology of sensations, perceptions, ideas, attitudes, and feelings of which an individual or a group is aware at any given time or within a period.

For many years, scientists have tried to figure out the connection between consciousness and the Laws of the Universe. Some believe the two are interconnected, while others label the idea as quackery. Following a vast pool of debates and studies, the truth behind the conscious mind and its connection to the Universe has remained a mystery. What science has discovered is that humans have an innate connection to the energy of the Universe, and, with conscious awareness, can determine their level of health, and manifest physical reality.

Consciousness is the collaborative process in which every organ and cell in your body operates, driven by your thoughts and emotions. Negative experiences create negative thoughts and emotions, disrupting the body and making you vulnerable to illness and disease. Consciousness connects you not only to every other living thing on this planet but also to the Universe itself, ultimately forming everything you experience and influencing how you view the world. Opiate consumption causes a loss in your connection to the environment, reality, and your true self, which essentially is your consciousness.

You feel disconnected from the rest of the world because in every way - mentally, physically, spiritually, and emotionally - you are. Your false ego self is doing fine while your genuine soul or consciousness has lost its connection entirely. Opiates support your ego by altering your mind and suppressing emotional, mental, and physical pain and trauma. The second the drug wears off, negative feelings that have been bottled up rush back in, creating a vicious cycle. These drugs only provide temporary relief from painful thoughts and emotions, and the true nature of the problem is never addressed or dealt with properly. Until problems are faced and their energy released, they will never permanently go away. The longer they are pushed down, the more they affect a person's psychological and emotional stability, creating many other health problems in the future. Your subconscious mind carries memories of everything you have ever experienced throughout your life, and they still affect you. Finding some way to release these past negative experiences will start the healing process and lead you down the path to enlightenment and freedom from opiate addiction.

Most modern treatment methods aim towards treating the symptoms and not the underlying cause of the problem. During detox, the focus is primarily geared at relieving you of uncomfortable withdrawal symptoms and cravings. The reason most people chronically relapse following treatment is because the underlying problem that initially caused the person to start using opiates in the first place is completely ignored. Negative feelings and emotional trauma remain dormant in your subconscious mind. Although you are completely unaware of it and might not even remember any of your past negative experiences, they are still affecting you and are the core reason for your drug problem.

Humans thrive with connection, and each possess an innate need to be seen and heard. Opiate addiction not only disconnects you consciously from reality and the world, but also prevents you from forming healthy bonds in personal relationships. Degrading stigmatism leaves you no other choice than to bond with people who possess similar interests as you. If you cannot find another human to bond with, you will accept anything that gives you a sense of security and acceptance - drugs.

Once you begin the recovery process and start taking your medication regularly, you will feel awake, aware, and alive again. Your conscious state of mind will be reestablished, connecting you with the oneness of all creation. Positive changes and thoughts create positive results meaning that intentions and desires will begin manifesting into your life. You are what you think about, and your thoughts affect your outcome. Whether you view this as God, the laws of Quantum Physics at work, or simply the natural flow of the Universe, it is a proven fact.

Many people are terrified that there is no way to stop once they become dependent on opiates, and if they do somehow manage to quit, that they have already caused irreversible damage to their brain and body. The excellent news is that if you have caused any internal damage from drug use, this miraculous vessel of ours is part of the whole Universe, connecting us with every other living thing. Your body has the built-in capability of healing and protecting itself from toxins and harmful stimuli each second you are alive and breathing. There are over 300 trillion cells in your body, that coherently communicate with one another. They operate through your level of consciousness which is dictated by your thoughts and emotions. Designed by the same Divine Intelligence that created all life, your body is always performing miracles, flowing in rhythmic harmony with every other living organism. Busy schedules and continuous mental conditioning cause us to forget the importance of these magnificent everyday miracles and lose sight of how powerful we really are.

One way you can erase negative mental conditioning and create harmony in your life is through a practice called mindfulness. This is a simple technique that has been practiced by ancient civilizations since humans were put on this planet. It was put on the back burner for hundreds of years and is just recently beginning to re-appear. Medical professionals have discovered a wide range of health benefits that can develop from a regular meditation practice.

A meta-analysis of over 500 studies found a significant association between higher states of consciousness and improvements in daily life. For example, researchers found that consciousness becomes correlated with increased self-actualization, creativity, intelligence, and cognitive-perceptual abilities. It also helps remove addictive behavior, anxiety, aggression, depression, and introversion. Moreover, higher states of consciousness promote moral sensitivity, faith, courage, personal force, sympathy, affection, and morality, while at the same time reducing fear, anger, and hatred.

Within the last few years, many religious luminaries and scientists have attributed their genius abilities to mindfulness. It is a secure, free service, that almost anyone can practice, and is known to promote good health and vitality without the use of modern medicine. Diseases thought to have caused irreversible damage were healed through mindfulness. Although there are many different types of meditation techniques available, the one thing they all offer is that they are all forms of mindfulness. The most common types of meditation practiced today are mantra, kundalini yoga, binaural beats, nature sounds, chakra balancing, and reiki healing sounds.

The amount of time you were using opiates will equal the amount of time it will probably take to heal your brain and start rebuilding your life, progressing towards a brighter future. Healing starts within the mind, with meditation eliminating negative mental conditioning caused by the shame and trauma of your opiate dependence. As your brain and body begin to heal, you will notice significant positive changes occurring in your life. Relationships will become more nurturing, stronger, reliable, and loving. Your perception of the world will no longer be clouded by the exhausting, never-ending search for a false antidote for pain. You will start to appreciate things like nature and knowledge, filling your mind with positive thoughts which will in turn produce positive emotions, crucial for your wellbeing.

Meditation will free you from feelings of exasperated anxiety, potentially overwhelming you because of the sudden onset of clarity. You have become so accustomed to the negativity surrounding your life created by your drug-induced lifestyle. These new feelings may seem unfamiliar or uncomfortable at first. Continue meditating, and it will relieve you of these negative emotions while at the same time exercising feelings of calmness, relaxation, contentment, and bliss. Positive thoughts and emotions will begin repairing areas of your brain damaged from long-term opiate abuse, allowing you to access and utilize their functions again.

Meditation was first made prominent in India and the Far East, with some of the earliest written records coming from the ancient Hindu teachings of Vedanta. This practice teaches that the inner self, spirit, soul, or "Atman" is the "first principle" or essence of the individual. Hinduism teaches that a person must acquire self-knowledge, realizing that one's true self is one and the same as the transcendent self, "Brahman."

Through meditation, you will become mindful, focusing your attention on an object, thought, or activity, achieving a mentally clear and emotionally calm, stable state. Mindfulness is known to increase peace, perception, self-confidence, and well-being, enabling a person to reconnect with that part of themselves that is inseparable from all that exists. Studies have shown it can restore neuropathways damaged from long term drug use. People who practice daily meditation are said to live longer and suffer from fewer health problems throughout their lives. They possess a calm, relaxed presence and can handle life's challenges more efficiently.

Most people hear about meditation but do not know where or how to start practicing it. They might anticipate that a regular meditation practice is out of reach or difficult to achieve. The truth is, meditation has become extremely popular recently, and there are classes and courses available nearly everywhere. The internet offers a wide variety of meditations to the public. Many of them are beneficial; an option that I found enjoyable and informative was Deepak Chopra's guided mantra meditations, either with him alone or the 21 Day Meditation Challenge with Deepak Chopra and Oprah Winfrey. It is free and easy to sign up on the Chopra Center Website, where they offer free 21 Day Meditation Challenges based on a variety of positive subject matters. Listening to these meditations will help you heal internally and lead you in the right direction for reaching your long-term recovery goals.

Ancient Hindu traditions teach that it is through the yoga of meditation an individual can reach advanced levels of conscious awareness. The answer to all human issues and misconceptions, is simply the process of uniting your conditioned ego-self who has a drug problem, with your immortal soul's true nature, which is free, unbounded, and eternal. Reconnecting with your soul will begin the healing process, enabling you to accept the fact that being a co-creator is every human's birthright. We are all equal and One with the Divine Intelligence who gave us life. Meditation can very quickly officiate your intentions toward recovery, transforming them into conscious reality.

POWER OF THE WORDS "I AM"

There are two specific words that have the power to deeply influence the outcome of your future. They are particularly common words, most people use throughout their day, not being aware of their significance. They are the words "I AM", and they have the power to transform any words following them into conscious physical reality. In the Bible, the Israelites referred to God as "The God of our forefathers" or "The God of Abraham." However, at the time, there was no specific name for the Divine creator. Then one day, Moses, still just a poor shepherd, came upon a burning bush which the fire did not consume. A voice spoke to him from within the flames and said he must go before the Pharaoh and demand the release of the Israelite slaves. When Moses asked who he should say sent him, the voice answered: "I AM that I AM." This is the first account in history of the creator force having a name. Armed with the power of God's name, Moses went on to manifest some of the greatest miracles ever told in the Bible.

Religious authorities, seeing the power that came from uttering the words, "I AM that I AM," charged anyone who spoke it with the highest form of blasphemy. Therefore, throughout the ages, its strength has always been unrecognized, misinterpreted, and misunderstood.

The words I AM later became known as the most powerful words in the human language. People found that it did not matter what style or culture they are spoken in. Any words that come after "I AM," will quickly manifest into your life, and create your physical reality. This concept is one of The Law of Attraction's most famous teachings. For example, if someone is constantly thinking or speaking about how miserable their life is and express it by saying, "I AM so miserable," then they will continue to have negative experiences in their life. If the wording is changed into a more positive affirmation like, "I AM so happy I AM no longer miserable," then they will soon see positive changes taking place. The key is to become consciously aware of your thoughts and words, realizing that the vibrational frequencies they create - whether positive or negative - hold significant power in determining the outcome of your future.

LOST GOSPELS OF THOMAS

Thousands of years after the Bible was written, archeologists discovered a jar filled with written scrolls, that was buried deep inside an early Egyptian tomb at *Nag Hammadi*. Nearly every text found was written in the ancient Coptic language, and they all followed the Gnostic traditions - meaning they teach salvation through wisdom and mystical knowledge. Gnosticism teaches that people are all souls in material bodies, and only through actual experience, can they ascend. They believe that Jesus is the redeemer, who came to teach knowledge and liberate mankind. He communicated this knowledge to select individuals, one of whom went on to write The Gospel of Thomas, which was one of the works discovered at Nag Hammadi. If this text, lost for almost two thousand years, were to be placed in the modern Bible, the message about the power that is held within each human would be revealed.

The Gospel of Thomas does not tell a story but is rather a compilation of approximately 114 sayings attributed to Jesus. The opening words of the text reads:

"These are the secret words which Jesus, the Living One spoke, and Didymus Judas Thomas wrote down. And he said, 'Whosoever finds the interpretation of these sayings shall never taste death. Let not him who seeks desist until he finds. When he finds he will be troubled, when he is troubled, he will marvel, and he will reign over the Universe.'"

The written sayings themselves are not the secret. The secret lies in their interpretation. When you find the correct answers, it will trouble you at first, because it goes against everything you have been conditioned to believe. When the truth sets in, it will marvel you, and then you will know your own personal power and come to realize that you have supreme reign over your life and everything in it. It is then that you can truly experience heaven on Earth whenever you so choose.

The Gospel of Thomas is eliminated from the Bible; Western religion claims that if you read it and compare it to what you see in the New Testament, it is a very different kind of book describing an entirely different Jesus. World religions claim that these teachings about Jesus mesh with individual philosophical principals that only grew in popularity and therefore are not necessary to the works of the Bible.

There was a time when Western tradition taught this field and the language of emotion as part of common knowledge. These teachings were in our texts until the year 325 AD, at which time they were edited to coincide with church teachings. We lost tremendous amounts of useful information when this happened. In the early Christian church, Emperor Constantine decided which words in the Bible to keep and which ones to eliminate from society. At least 45 books were either entirely taken away, or fully edited to go along with the fearful dogma that was being impressed upon a mostly illiterate audience. The fundamental knowledge that was meant to be passed on to all humans has been either hidden or changed drastically, and only a select few know the truth behind this sacred universal knowledge. The Gospel of Thomas teaches that just because each person is individually unique does not make us separate. We are all a part of the same universal consciousness, merely taking on different forms, and therefore will always rediscover this wisdom, regardless of how deep it is buried!

Here are some of the sayings by Jesus that were found in The Gospels of Thomas, as well as some of their interpretations:

Verse 3: "If those who lead you say to you, 'See the kingdom is in the sky,' then the birds of the sky will precede you. If they say to you, 'It is in the sea,' then the fish will precede you. Rather, the kingdom is inside of you and it is outside of you. When you come to know yourselves, then you will become known, and you will realize it is you who are the sons of the living Father. But if you will not know yourselves, you will dwell in poverty, and it is you who are that poverty."

Interpretation: This teaching refers to the consequences of believing that the power is outside of the individual. If you think that ruling power belongs to someone or something else other than yourself, then that is what will hold dominion over your life. When you realize that you are part of the one universal collective consciousness that moves through everything, and that all your power comes from within, you can begin living life in an ascended and productive way. 'The kingdom is inside of you, and it is outside of you,' means that you literally manifest your circumstances from within. 'If you do not know yourselves, you dwell in poverty, and it is you who is that poverty.' This reveals that outside events and people can influence your life, mentally conditioning you in a negative way that keeps you from living the richness that is your birthright.

Verse 27: "If you do not fast from the world, you will not find the (Father's) domain."
Interpretation: If we do not turn away from negative circumstances and start to believe that the power to bring about all changes comes from within; we will continue to experience that reality in our lives.

Verse 48: "If (thought and emotion) make peace with each other in this one house (you), They will say to the mountain, "Move away," and it will move away."
Interpretation: Here, Jesus is portraying to us the power we have when we combine our thoughts with our emotions.

Verse 50: "If they say to you, 'Where did you come from?' say to them, 'We came from the light, the place where the light came into being on its own accord and established itself and became manifest through their image.' If they say to you, 'Is it you?' say, 'We are Its children, we are the elect of the living Father.' If they ask you, 'What is the sign of your Father in you?' say to them, 'It is movement and repose.'"
Interpretation: The word light is used to portray the origin of humans and represents the consciousness inside each one of us, manifested as a physical being. It is the all in all, that exists in everyone. Consciousness lives through us in the form of activity and awareness.

Verse 77: "Jesus said, "It is I who AM the Light which is above them all. It is I who AM the all. From me did the all come forth, and unto me did the all extend. Split a piece of wood, and I AM there. Lift up the stone, and you will find me there."

Interpretation: This explains that one consciousness lives within everything. What lives in Jesus also lives within all other living things, including all humans.

Verse 106: "When you make the two (thought and emotion) one, you will say to the mountain, "Mountain move away," and the mountain will move away."

Interpretation: When you can combine your thoughts and your emotions into one single powerful force of energy, you will gain the confidence to speak to the world and make a positive difference towards benefiting the greater good of mankind. When thoughts and emotions become one in our hearts, we create the feelings in our bodies.

Verse 113: "His disciples said to him, "When will the kingdom come?" Jesus said, "It will not come by waiting for it. It will not be a matter of saying, 'here it is' or 'there it is.' Rather, the kingdom of the Father is spread out upon the Earth, and men do not see it."

Interpretation: We have always had the power within us but have lost sight of it. It is not something that we have to wait to experience. This consciousness is already a part of all things, including each one of us.

These ancient teachings reveal to us that there is a universal energy field we can utilize with the power of spoken language. In the early Christian Bible, there is a famous passage that says, "Ask, and you shall receive." To request, we must speak to the Divine energy field in the language that it understands. The field does not recognize our voice, it recognizes the power of our heart. When we have a feeling, our heart creates electrical, magnetic waves of energy that is the language the Divine field understands. When you create the atmosphere in your heart as if it has already come into fruition, and you have faith in the fact that it really exists, electric magnetic waves are produced, and after joining this Divine energy field will soon manifest into conscious reality.

In the edited version of the King James Bible, in John 16: 23, 24, it says:

"Whatever ye ask the Father in my name, he will giveth to you. Hitherto have ye asked nothing in my name. Ask, and ye shall receive that your joy may be full."

This edited version, rewritten in the 4th century, has taken the part out that tells us how to ask for what we want. In the unedited original Aramaic version, it reveals the two imperative sentences that were removed. It says:

"All things that you ask straightly, directly from inside my name, you will be given. So far, you have not done this. Ask without hidden motive and be surrounded by your answer. Be enveloped by what you desire, that your gladness be made full."

This scripture is not implying that you should speak words when asking for what you want, but that you should be surrounded and feel as if your answer has already happened. This is when your thoughts and emotions have become one. Ask without hidden motive means to ask without judgment. Ask without the right or wrong or the good or bad. Ask without the ego. Ask from the heart, and it is promised that you shall receive everything you desire.

To utilize this Divine power towards putting an end to your opiate addiction, you must not judge your condition as right or wrong, good or bad – it is simply what it is, a condition of living as natural and acceptable as daylight or rain. Accept your addiction as one of many possibilities because, in the quantum world, all things are possible. Do not say to yourself, "Bad addiction, you must go away." First accept your addiction as it is without any hidden motive or judgment. You must say, "Now I AM going to choose a new reality by feeling as if I AM already healed from my addiction." Physical reality will respond to the language it understands and heal you. This is an emotion that comes from your heart and not your mind.

The Gospel of Thomas represents our connection to consciousness and all that is, and carries within it's pages the knowledge that will free mankind. If a person does not experience this higher state of consciousness because they are consumed by mind-altering substances, they start to believe they are separate, alone, and merely a victim of circumstance. To break free from any manifested reality not serving your desires, your false image of self must be replaced by the power that you truly possess.

CHAPTER VIII

Reflective Power

"The eyes are the mirror of the soul and reflect everything that seems to be hidden, and like a mirror, they also reflect the person looking into them."
—*Paulo Coelho*

Manifestation of life on this planet was made possible with the use of brilliantly reflective electromagnetic energy particles of bio photonic light. This reflective power flows through all living organisms, providing the perfect energy source, while efficiently sustaining growth and survival on our planet. In the Bible, in the book of Genesis it tells us:

"In the beginning, God created the heavens and the Earth. Now the Earth was formless and desolate, and there was darkness upon the surface of the waters. And God said, "Let there be light." Then there was light. After that, God saw that the light was good, and God began to divide the light from the darkness. God called the light Day and the darkness he called Night. And there was evening, and there was morning, the first day."

The following verses go on to say:

"God went on to create the man in His image. In His image, He created him, male and female He created them... And God went on to form the man out of dust from the ground and to blow into his nostrils the breath of life, and the man became a living person."

These scriptures reveal that God used the elemental energies of sound, light, air, and earth to create our Universe and everything in it. He created us in His image, giving us the innate ability to become co-creators, processing our manifestations like Him using the power of energy.

Around 450 B.C., the ancient Greeks produced the belief that there are four elements every living thing is made from: earth, water, air, and fire. This theory was later supported and added to by Aristotle, who suggested that there was also a fifth element, called *aether*, or *quintessence*. He was taught by one of the greatest philosophers and teachers of his time, Plato, that *aether* is the material that fills the region of the Universe above the terrestrial sphere. It is believed that this very rarefied, and highly elastic substance, permeates all space, including the interstices between the particles of matter. It is also the medium whose vibrations constitute light and other electro-magnetic radiation. Many popular theories used the concept of *aether* to explain natural phenomena, such as the traveling of light and gravity.

Ancient civilizations were well aware of the power of reflection and the waves of energy fluctuating throughout and around the human body. They also knew the importance behind these colorful energy waves of light for obtaining a spiritual connection and allowing humans the ability to co-create. The ancients precisely knew how to entangle their energy frequency with that of the Universe, which is the key to making manifestation possible.

One way to witness the natural expression of the powerful Law of Reflection, is in a rainbow stretching itself across the heavens, during or following a heavy rainfall. The straight vibrant rays emitting from the sun must precisely hit the back of a raindrop to cause a magnificent prism of colorful light to fan out across the sky. The rainbow has always been symbolic of luck and good fortune. Many other mystical representations have been associated with its incredible stream of energy, bowing over us and gracing us with its presence. The colors of the rainbow are the same colors represented by the seven chakras in the human body, as well as the human aura.

Several chakras are located throughout the body; however, the seven main energy centers are positioned from the base of the spine to the crown of the head. These primary energy centers help the body regulate all biological processes, from organ function to the immune system, as well as balancing the emotional body. An aura is an electromagnetic vibration emanating from all living things, whose brightness and color is deeply connected to one's chakra health. The trained naked eye can view this energy spectrum, though it is easier when under individual ultraviolet light sensors. These energy waves extend about a foot from the body and appear as luminous shades of the rainbow, glowing around the shoulders and top of the head. Auras can explain details about someone's personality as well as reveal possible health concerns.

Light is often said to reflect off of mirrors and other smooth surfaces such as the surface of water. The reason this happens is because of the fact that light is an extremely fast-moving type of energy. It does not only reflect off of mirrors, but in reality light reflects off of everything. Look around the room you're sitting in. You may see chairs, other people, perhaps some paintings on the wall. Light is reflecting off of all these objects. When the reflected light hits your eyes, your brain translates it into images that you recognize as the things around you. Light is made up of many rays, or beams, of energy. Ordinarily, many rays of light hit an object at the same time. Upon hitting the object, the rays of light are reflected in different directions. When the reflected rays hit our eyes, we see the object they are reflecting off of.

Seeing your reflection in the mirror is something so common that you might take it for granted, but there is a lot to consider just lurking under the surface. When light rays hit a mirror, they are reflected perfectly. The reflected rays therefore meet at a point. This phenomenon, which is called convergence, causes us to see reflected images when the light rays hit our eyes. When light hits a flat mirror, it is also reflected off of our bodies. The rays that are refracted from our bodies then hit the mirror at varying angles and are reflected back perfectly.

Before mirrors adorned the walls of homes across the world, ancient civilizations observed their reflections in still pools of water or vessels made from clay filled with seemingly dark water. According to ancient legend, the first mirror formed in the Himalayas, where a little brook came to rest, laying still as if to ponder and reflect upon its course. When the first woman came along, she looked down into the tranquil pool and was surprised to see another girl! She slowly began to realize the other girl was merely a reflection of herself.

The long, controversial history of mirrors carries with it a spiritual nature that is far more mysterious and valuable, than most people realize. Typically used today for grooming and sustaining the satisfaction of vanity, the genuine history of these strange objects dates back to the beginning of human civilization. To the ancients, "mirror gazing" was an art that usually carried with it a spiritual or ceremonial significance. Reflection was personified with the human soul, and they believed that by observing it, one could transition to higher levels of consciousness. Mirrors were mainly used for spiritual advancement, performing magic and divination, soul reflection, gazing into other dimensions, foretelling the future, and communicating with the spirit world.

The first evidence of the fabrication of a reflective object was found in Anatolia, Turkey, dating as far back as 6000 BC. Ancient Turks sat in their tiny mud-brick huts, working with their hands for long hours, briskly polishing stones of black volcanic glass. They would rub the sharp objects until their fingers were raw, and the rocks shined like glistening black diamonds, revealing a reflection when held up to the sun. Satisfied that they had just created something magical, these beautiful shiny handmade mirrors became used as spiritual emblems, adorning the graves of beloved mothers, sisters, and daughters.

It was not until the year 1960 that archeologists discovered six of these obsidian mirrors and were surprised to find a civilization known to be simple hunter-gatherers to be so concerned with appearance. Upon studying the geographic location, they concluded these strange reflective objects were likely used by shamans during ritualistic ceremonies, as many of them were found in or near tombs.

Three millennia after the Anatolians laid the groundwork, the ancient Egyptians mastered the art of reflection. Somewhere between 3,000 and 4,000 BC, they began constructing round mirrors from highly-polished, flattened sheets of copper. Most of them were hand-held, with wooden and ivory handles, and had symbols etched on the front of them representing the sun god Ra. Egyptians considered the mirror to be a porthole to the "inner self" or soul. They used reflective energy to communicate with the spirit world and contact deceased relatives. They believed the past, present, and future could be seen through a mirror, practicing a technique known as "scrying" which is still used today. The mirror gave them direct access to other dimensions, and the worlds of the gods, while at the same time granting them the power to transcend to higher levels of consciousness and even immortality.

Thousands of years later, the Mayans – active from 250 to 1000 AD – would continue this tradition by burying mirrors with their deceased. Contemporary researchers believe that reflective artifacts were used as mystical devices by elite individuals for divinatory scrying. Ancient Mayans understood reflection as a window into an alternate dimension, a place where their gods and ancestors both dwelled. They believed this "other world" was filled with powerful forces, hidden from sight yet highly influential.

Ancient China also celebrated the light-enhancing properties of mirrors. For them, mirrors were tools of both physical observations as well as spiritual protection. The Chinese practice of manufacturing metal mirrors began around 4,000 years ago with circular bronze mirrors, polished to a shine on one side. The other side was inscribed with intricate pictographs depicting animals real and imagined, significant plants and flowers, and symbolic references that translate to "sunlight" or "clear and bright." Expensive and adored, these natural objects were owned by the wealthy few. The Chinese also utilize mirrors in their art of Feng shui, as mirrors shift the flow of energy in a room.

Despite imperfections found in early mirrors, they were considered wondrous instruments by our ancestors. They allowed humans not only to discover their image and become familiar with themselves, but also gave them the ability to use the visible to perceive the invisible. Sight was believed to be a favorable means for acquiring knowledge – literally the origins of the term, "I'll believe it when I see it" – and only through sight could one truly experience the beautiful. The mirror was regarded with exceptional symbolic importance because of its ability to enhance visual acuity while radiating light.

Folklore and superstitious beliefs associated with the mirror filled the ears and minds of curious listeners for many centuries. Following the fall of Rome, the Middle Ages began in Europe, at which time Christianity started to develop and became the sovereign ideology for most of the European population. The church taught that gazing at one's reflection was linked to the witchcraft, sorcery, and paganism, which were all forbidden practices associated with the devil. With the absence of reflection came the Dark Ages, an era marked by death and misery that lasted over five hundred years. The mirror became part of the religious vocabulary which developed its symbolic meanings from authoritative writings, Neoplatonic texts, and writings of the church fathers. The use of the mirror for self-transformation became forgotten in these texts because the church saw the mirror image as either a reflection of God or an instrument of the devil.

Towards the end of the Middle Ages, the underpinnings of Catholicism gave rise to the teachings of ancient Greek thinkers like Plotinus and Timaeus. From the latter, the church fathers derived a belief in metaphysics of light and reflection. The visible world was the image of the invisible and was believed to be the reflection of the Divine. Plotinus, the founder of Neoplatonism and generally regarded as one of the most influential philosophers of antiquity, reiterates the idea of a universally organized hierarchy as the basis for mystical reasoning. He considered the evident world to be a reflection emanating from the world of eternal forms. He also suggested that the human body is a reflection the soul makes visible after coming into direct contact with matter. Similar to when humans encounter a polished surface, a reflection becomes visible.

These teachings made way for a spiritual awakening leading to the birth of the Renaissance era. The mirror and its ancient reflective and mystical powers were brought back into consciousness alongside alchemy and Hermetic teachings. As an omnipresent metaphor in all spiritual literature, the mirror owed its influence to the optical sciences, which rose to prominence among the sciences of this time, as did the art of glassmaking. From the twelfth to the fourteenth century, the optical teachings of Robert Grosseteste became the influential core of a new movement. This was led by the *Franciscan School of Oxford*, which regarded specular vision as a privileged mode of knowledge.

According to Grosseteste, the entire world is of luminous essence, and rays of light are the first form of physical matter; thus, all activity initially consists of reflection. In this work, the figure of nature, taking up the mechanics of rainbows, draws a parallel between the colored reflections it issues forth through atmospheric turbulence, and the illusions that affect men. Just as the rays of the sun produce forms and colors by crossing the water and the clouds, the same rays, when they encounter the moods and instincts of man, create chaos in the soul, like the pain caused by love. He taught that first, a man must look at his reflection in the rolled waters of the "perilous fountain," then he must see himself in the "fountain of life," in which he sees a three faceted gemstone. It is a trinitarian light that no shadow can dim, and that does not require light from the sun to become illuminated since it is itself is a splendid source of light. This interpretation is a metaphor, in which man will finally enjoy the perfect vision and actual knowledge of life.

The mirror is boldly considered to be a reflective art of illusion that not only simulates the beauty of nature, but is also capable of inventing forms and rediscovering the process of creation. Grosseteste taught that when an object plunged into darkness is reflected in a luminous mirror, it is better recognized by its image than by its reality, bringing knowledge of what is to get done. This way of thinking opened a new chapter driven by a more mystical and enlightened outlook, allowing the mirror and its powerful reflective energy to find its way back into the hearts and souls of humanity.

At the dawn of the 14th century, glass mirrors started to replace metal ones. They became a sought-after luxury that only extremely wealthy people or royals could afford. The first great glass mirrors originated from the Italian island of Murano, located in the Venetian lagoon. The glassmakers of Murano jealously guarded the tricks of their trade; so too did the Venetian government, who, anxious to keep this art local, made spilling trade secrets punishable by death. The Venetian Republic treated glassworkers more like artists then artisans, carefully protecting and monitoring them; it also granted them many privileges, such as the right to marry the daughters of nobles.

For centuries, Venetian mirrors were considered the height of luxury, so of course, everyone in France wanted one. A Venetian mirror framed in a rich border of silver was worth more than a painting by Raphael, the mirror costing 8,000 pounds (approximately $14,000,000 by today's standards!) and the picture costing only 3,000. With mirrors in such high demand, anyone who could introduce the industry to France was promised a generous reward, both by King Louis XIV and by the mirror-obsessed population residing there. In the early 1660s, the king's finance minister was finally able to successfully lure several glassmakers away from Murano and start a competing workshop, specializing in the manufacturing of glass mirrors.

A couple of years later, two of Murano's leading artisans died suddenly, one from a fever, and the other from mysterious stomach pains. As suspicion arose, fear began seeping into the minds of surviving glassmakers. In 1670 the French royalty backed company finally figured out how to blow, flatten, and coat large polished panes of glass. With the unveiling of Versailles's Hall of Mirrors in 1684, it was apparent that the carefully hidden secrets of mirror making had escaped Murano. The monopoly was broken, and from this point on, glass mirrors were more commonplace and cheaper. When mirrors were considered rare and costly, they were often symbolic of the Sacred and Divine. As they started to become more commonplace, they lost their mystical flare and became associated with the egotistical satisfaction of vanity and the processes of everyday grooming.

And so, the simple glass mirror helped shape the modern secular age. It is referred to as "one of mankind's most consistent civilizers," bringing to those who look upon it a sense of personal reflection and comparative identity. The mirror goes above and beyond in proving itself to be central in every aspect of modern technological advancement, while at the same time being advantageous to a wide range of industries across the world. The mirror appears throughout human history as a tool for either self-knowledge or self-delusion. Reflective surfaces are used to reveal and hide reality and have greatly influenced philosophy, literature, art, religion, folklore, magic, and science. With the invention of cheap industrialized glass and new modern methods of applying reflective properties, mirrors have become everyday objects even in the poorest of homes.

The long, mysterious, and somewhat controversial history of mirrors is also the history of the study of light. Light is a medium which acts simultaneously as a wave particle, imposing a speed limit on the Universe, and in a sense, "is the Universe," according to Einstein – as in his famous equation, "$E=mc^2$", which literally means "the energy of a material object is calculated by multiplying it's mass by the speed of light squared." If all matter is merely energy condensed to a slow vibration and is so intricately connected to the speed of light, the true importance of Einstein's work is revealed as a proof that everything in the universe is made of light!

A field of electromagnetic radiation is produced when you run electricity through a magnet. This field is invisible to the naked eye until it hits dust particles in the air, revealing that it travels in straight lines. Visible light, from red to violet, is only one octave in a spectrum which ranges from mile-long radio waves (past infrared) to high-energy bursts of Gamma rays (past ultraviolet). Modern science has figured out a way to make unusual mirrors capable of reflecting most of those wavelengths as well.

The human body is a constant flow of thousands of chemically organic synergy mechanisms, connecting molecules, cells, organs, and fluids, throughout the brain and nervous system. Up until recently, scientists believed that every interaction between cells operates in a specific sequence. They thought messages were passed on similar to when a runner passes the baton to the next runner during a race. Recently however, through extensive research at the International Institute of Biophysics, Fritz-Albert Popp has put forth the hypothesis that bio photons emit from a coherent electrodynamic field within the human body. He concludes that each of the 300 trillion cells in our body communicates with each other coherently through bio photonic emissions.

One of Dr. Popp's close colleagues, the late Dr. Mae Wan Hoe, physicist, scientist, lecturer, author, and founder of The Institute of Science in Society, is best known for her pioneering work on the physics of organisms and sustainable systems. She describes how the living organism, including the human body, is "coherent beyond our wildest dreams." She explains how every part of our body is "in communication with every other part through a dynamic, tunable, and responsive, liquid crystalline medium, pervading the entire body, from organs, and tissues, to the interior of every cell." The "liquid crystalline matrix" she refers to is water, which is an ideal transmitter for communication, resonance, and coherence.

The logic of physics explains consciousness as the most advanced part of the universal creative process. In the same way, physics is used to describe modern electronics. Since this is considered the most basic form of science, conscious awareness and free will as a physical process are also explained this way. This theory explains free will by pointing out that the Universe is a continuum based on one universal method of energy exchange, which coincides with atoms of the Periodic Table. It is never at absolute zero, meaning there is always a spontaneous absorption and emission of light or photon energy. If our eyes were more sensitive to the different wavelengths of light, we would be able to see that everything is continuously radiating electromagnetic waves. This energy is referred to as "the great dance of creation." Each photon vibrates just once, but the process of energy exchange is always creating the ever-changing world of everyday life humans measure as time.

Atoms are continually interacting with the electromagnetic spectrum, or what we commonly refer to as light. With the exchange of bio photonic energy, a positive and negative charge is created. When commonly known objects touch and interact with one another, it is because an electrical charge comes into contact. Every movement we make, and every thought we think, creates an exchange of photonic vibrational frequencies.

Communication of cells creates ripples in the fabric of space-time, forming its revolutionary path relative to the energy and momentum of its actions. For free will to exist, as part of a process explained by physics, one of the most fundamental things we need is uncertainty. This is made possible when light interacts with the electron probability cloud, encompassing each atom. When the energy from the light is absorbed, it gets spontaneously emitted and builds a wave function with an uncertainty, mathematically represented by Heisenberg's Uncertainty Principle of 1901. In this theory, it is the same uncertainty we have with any future event at the smallest scale of the creative process, considered to be the surpassing or continuum of time. When electromagnetic radiation, or light, interacts with an atom, a photon electron coupling forms, with the movement of positive and negative charge. This process represents a future that unfolds photon by photon, with the wave-particle duality of light and matter in the form of electrons. This enables us to work with a blank canvas, using consciousness to transform possibilities into actual occurrences.

By explaining conscious awareness in its purest form as electrical energy in the brain, coherent of its electrical capabilities, consciousness becomes the most advanced part of one whole universal process. Electrical energy, relative to the structure of the brain, instinctually creates chemical reactions and changes in our cells. Chemical energy is stored in the bones, where atoms are held together. As bones form and break, a constant exchange of bio-photonic energy takes place, with the future unfolding to the electrical activity and normal function of the brain. This is a universal process with the future always unfolding relative to the structure of atoms, and the wavelength of light.

The most fundamental component of consciousness is electrical activity in the brain. Conscious awareness is formed by the electrical potential remaining in the present moment, in the center of its reference frame. We have an infinite amount of dynamic, interactive reference frames that create our Universe, continually coming in and out of existence. Each of these reference frames has a timeline from the past into the future. It is in the personalization of the brain being in the present moment, and centering its frame of reference, that gives us the concept of "mind." This forms within each one of us, our own personal view of the Universe. This process is based entirely on cause and effect. Consciousness is always at the forefront of the creative process; therefore, by changing your thought process, you can co-create the life you have always wanted.

The possibility of time-travel is a common belief. In this theory, the atoms of the Periodic Table form their space-time as part of a single universal process of continuous creation. Life is an integral part of nature, with the flow of time being a process of constant energy exchange. Our consciousness becomes a constant stream of an unbroken, ever-changing fluctuation of our ideas, feelings, dreams, hopes, and emotions. What this means is that our conscious awareness is part of that same universal process.

The main effect this has on humans is the aging process. A past that is never changing, and a future existing primarily as a probability function, or Quantum Wave-Particle Function is then formed. A creative interactive process occurs, with the future unfolding alongside the energy and momentum of our actions. Art, poetry, music, and mathematics are all examples of this. In physics, humans are all connected by one universal, physical process, with electromagnetism interacting with the atoms of the Periodic Table. The oneness that becomes filled by meditation is based on the same process and forms the unity of physics and mathematics, which ancient civilizations were aware of all along.

The eyes are often referred to as the windows or mirrors of the soul. This famous metaphor is used to explain how a person's thoughts are ascertained by looking deep into their eyes, but it goes much further than this. Similar phrases are used throughout history, the earliest reference dating back to the Bible. In Mathew 6: 22, Jesus said to his disciples:

"The eye is the lamp of the body. If your eyes are healthy, your whole body will be full of light. But if your eyes are unhealthy, your whole body will be full of darkness. If then, the light within you is darkness, how great is that darkness?"

Around 106 BC, Cicero said, "the face is a picture of the mind as the eyes are its interpreter." A famous Latin proverb states: "The face is the index of the mind." The French have said for centuries, "The eyes are the mirror of the soul."

When two people gaze deeply into each other's eyes, a spark ignites. Each of them feels an innate, deep connection, so compelling that it might feel as if they can see through to the depths of each other's soul, metaphorically speaking, of course. They experience an intense connection to one another on a mental, emotional, and spiritual level. They almost feel as though they are looking through a spiritual porthole, leading directly to the depths of their inner self, while defenses and insecurities seem to break away.

Deep eye gazing has psychological benefits for each person as well. It changes their perception and allows them to experience feelings of empathy towards one another, due to their cognitive attributes becoming stimulated. They begin to feel like they can understand each other on a much deeper, emotional level. It is almost as if gazing deeply into a person's eyes allows you to feel their pain, happiness, anger, or any other emotion they may be experiencing. Wisdom, or the lack thereof, can also be determined by looking deep into the eyes of another. You can usually discern whether they have experienced a lifetime of pain and sorrow, or if joy and laughter have filled most of their days.

The human nervous system controls eye function and facial expressions. This intricate part of the human anatomy coordinates its actions, and sensory information, by transmitting signals to and from different parts of the body. The nervous system detects changes in the environment having a direct influence on the body, then works with the endocrine system to respond to such events. The nervous system consists of two main parts: the central nervous system, which is the spinal cord and the brain, and the peripheral nervous system, which is mainly a cluster of several different nerve cells and fibers. The peripheral nervous system releases chemicals and transmits messages to the central nervous system, controlling organ functionality. The sympathetic nervous system is activated in cases of emergencies to mobilize energy. In contrast, the parasympathetic nervous system is activated when we are in a relaxed state.

When you find yourself in the darkness, you typically become nervous or on alert as your eyes are instinctually on the lookout for predators or anything else that could be a potential threat. Your heart rate begins to speed up, which causes the pupils to dilate, allowing you to have a broader view of your surroundings in case you encounter danger. This also enables you to find your way out of the darkness. Consumption of drugs like LSD, ecstasy, or methamphetamines, evokes heightened levels of excitement and arousal, and often times, nervousness, and anxiety start to creep in. The pupils begin to dilate because the chemical structure in these types of drugs overstimulates the nervous system. The exact opposite happens when the eyes become subjected to bright light. The brain then transmits a message to your nervous system, letting it know you are out of danger, and slowing down your heart rate. You are then put into a naturally relaxed mindset, and your pupils constrict, shrinking smaller.

The connection between reflection and your soul has been well known since antiquity. Combining ancient optical science with modern-day physics will help you understand how vision, sight, and sound, govern your connection to the Universe. This allows you to manifest your thoughts into matter. Deeply gazing into your own eyes, while looking at your reflection in a mirror, has the same effect as intimately looking deep into the eyes of another person. This practice, commonly known as "mirror work," or "mirror magic," is a simple technique that has been referred to as, "the most powerful tool in the Universe," and is proven to quickly manifest dreams into reality. Modern day science is just beginning to uncover the vital role conscious awareness plays in "mind over matter" and the natural universal process of creation.

CHAPTER IX

Life in the Fast(ing) Lane

"The best of all medicines is resting and fasting."
—*Benjamin Franklin*

Fasting has been used for thousands of years and is one of the oldest therapies in medicine. Many of the great doctors of ancient times and the oldest healing systems throughout history, have recommended fasting as an integral method of healing and disease prevention. Hippocrates, the father of Western medicine, believed fasting enabled the body to heal itself. 500 years ago, Paracelsus, another great healer in Western tradition, wrote: "Fasting is the greatest remedy, the physician within." Ayurvedic medicine has long advocated fasting as one of its primary treatment methods. In ancient Greece, Pythagoras was one among many who professed the virtues of fasting. During the 14th century, fasting was practiced by St. Catherine of Siena. Fasting in one form or another is a distinguished tradition, and throughout the centuries it has been claimed to have brought about physical and spiritual renewal.

In primitive cultures, a fast was often demanded before going to war, or as part of a coming-of-age ritual. It was used to assuage angry spirits by native North Americans, and as a rite to avoid catastrophes such as famine. Fasting has played a vital role in all the world's major religions, being associated with penance and other forms of self-control. Judaism has several annual fasting days, including Yom Kippur, the Day of Atonement. In Islam, Muslims fast during the holy month of Ramadan, while Roman Catholics and Eastern Orthodoxy observe a 40 day fast during Lent. This custom is to signify the period when Jesus fasted for 40 days in the desert.

During the 14th century, surviving for periods without nourishment was regarded as a sign of holiness and purity. Julian of Norwich, an English recluse and mystic, used it as a means of communicating with Christ. In some tribal belief systems, the gods were thought to reveal their divine teaching in dreams and visions only after a fast by the temple priests. Fasting has also been used as a gesture of political protest, one classic example being the Suffragettes; another being Mahatma Gandhi, who undertook 17 fasts during the struggle for Indian independence. His most extended fast lasted 21 days. In 1942, he fasted again to draw attention to calls for Britain to leave India.

Gandhi was imprisoned on many occasions in both South Africa and India. He attempted to practice nonviolence and truth in all situations and advocated that others do the same. Gandhi lived modestly in a self-sufficient residential community and wore the traditional Indian dhoti and shawl, woven with yarn that was hand-spun on a charkha. He ate simple vegetarian food and undertook long fasts as a means of both self-purification and social protest.

In the 19th century, with medical supervision, therapeutic fasting was used to either treat or prevent ill health. This became part of the Natural Hygiene Movement in the United States. A revered pioneer of that movement was Dr. Herbert Shelton, who in 1928 opened Dr. Shelton's Health School in San Antonio, Texas. He claimed to have helped 40,000 patients recover their health with a water fast. Shelton wrote: "Fasting must be recognized as a fundamental and radical process that is older than any other mode of caring for the sick organism, for it is employed on the plane of instinct." Shelton was an advocate of alternative medicine, an author, pacifist, vegetarian, and a big believer in *rawism* and fasting for obtaining optimal health and longevity. In 1986, he was nominated by the American Vegetarian Party to run as a candidate for President of the United States. He viewed himself as the champion of the original Natural Hygiene ideas that started in the 1830s. His ideas have been described as quackery by critics.

In the UK, fasting became part of the "Nature Cure," an approach that also stressed the importance of exercise, diet, sunshine, fresh air, and positive thinking. Fasting in Great Britain was at its most popular in the 1920s. Tom Greenfield is a naturopath who now runs a clinic in Canterbury, England. This is the first Nature Cure clinic to offer fasting as a form of treatment. The clinic was first opened in Edinburgh, and some of their patients have been fasting there for many decades. Greenfield has used fasting to treat heart disease, high blood pressure, obesity, digestive problems, allergies, headaches, and many other health conditions.

Fasts were tailored to the patient's needs and could last anywhere from a day to a couple of months. People would have to first provide a full medical history background check to see if they were suitable candidates. Once approved, they would be closely monitored by a medical professional. Eventually scientific medicine became dominant as better drugs were developed, which caused fasting and the "Nature Cure" to fall out of favor in Britain."

In Germany, therapeutic fasting was pioneered by Dr. Otto Bachinger, and is still popular and offered at several clinics throughout the country. Many German hospitals run fasting weeks, funded by health insurance programs, to help manage obesity. In Germany, fasting is part of the *naturheilkundem*, translated in English as "the natural health practice." It has remained popular after becoming integrated into medical practice so patients could be referred for a fast through their doctors.

Fasting holidays held at centers and spas throughout Europe include Hungary, the Czech Republic, and Austria, and are growing in popularity. Recently, interest in fasting has revived in the UK and the United States. Millions of people attest to the many health benefits associated with intermittent fasting. This includes fasts such as the 5:2 diet or modified fasts, where only certain foods or juices are taken for a certain period. According to Greenfield, "If people can do a one day fast for a minimum of twice a year, maybe one in spring and one in autumn, setting aside a day they can rest, when they just drink water, this will help mitigate the toxic effects of daily living."

Fasting has also gained popularity in Western medicine over the past several decades as well, and many doctors feel it is beneficial for good health. Fasting is a central therapy in detoxification, a healing method founded on the principle that the buildup of toxic substances in the body is responsible for many illnesses and conditions.

Addiction is one perfect example of a chronic health condition that can be eliminated by doing a 24-hour, pure water fast. If you allow yourself to consume nothing but water within the 24-hour time period before you take your first dose of Buprenorphine and Naloxone, you will eliminate toxic buildup resulting from long-term opiate abuse. Your body will begin to eliminate built-up internal toxicity, assisting you in a speedy recovery process.

Addictions are composed of both physical and emotional elements. Opiates affect you physically, by causing changes in your biochemistry. This causes your body to demand more of the given substance to sustain homeostasis. Emotionally, addictive substances manipulate the way you relate to food, drink, or drugs by playing on the ego's tendency to become attached to objects in the world around you. In short, you feel you need the given substance, dragging you into a downward spiral with seemingly no way out.

Water fasting works like a "reset," helping to bring addictive cravings quickly and successfully to an end, as your body's healing metabolism catalyzes and intensifies the natural process of detox. Fasting is the ultimate form of "cold turkey" because the biochemical cycles which cause dependence are cut short in their tracks. This means that, in order to reduce any unpleasant withdrawal symptoms, it is usually a good idea to try to reduce the consumption of opiates (or any other mind-altering substances) prior to a water fast. If you use a water fast specifically to tackle a physical addiction, tapering the given substance before the fast can help. Withdrawal symptoms are inevitable and, unfortunately, are the price you pay for any addiction. Symptoms produced by opiate withdrawal are mental, emotional, and physical, causing severe flu-like symptoms, cold sweats, chills, achy muscles, fever, vomiting, and the intense emotions of a significant personal loss. Although these symptoms can be uncomfortable – themselves capable of causing anxiety, headaches, nausea, blurred vision, and severe mood swings - they are rarely dangerous.

Clearing the addictive substance from your body allows your endocrine/ hormonal system to adequately re-balance during the remainder of the water fast. Since you are not ingesting anything except pure water during this time, no external factors can influence what your body already knows is best for you.

Once you have succeeded and you are ready to start your medication, you will be able to see opiates for what they are; an evil poison that has been destroying your life. You should avoid opioids all together at this point. A successful water fast will reduce or even eliminate the temptation to fall back into wanting to take opioids in the first place. For the first time in probably a long time, you will be enjoying the gift of mother nature without the need for anything more. You will begin to enjoy the gift of food and life itself, possessing a newfound joy, free from the physical and emotional chains of addiction.

As important as any physical cleansing, water fasting also challenges you with emotional and spiritual blocks, bringing you face to face with your ego and fears. Your journey through water fasting mirrors your entire spiritual path. One of the most essential things in your spiritual development is how you relate to your ego. Your ego is that aspect of yourself that feels isolated and alone in the Universe and makes judgments about everyone and everything you come into contact with. It is this part of yourself that has fallen into opiate addiction.

Buddhists refer to this as the cycle of 'attachment and aversion.' By incessantly weighing up the world around you, you lose the ability simply to be, honestly accepting the world for how it is, without the need to try to control it. Your deeper self, soul, or consciousness is buried and lost beneath the ego's petty dramas, and a 24-hour water fast will help with restoration.

We all want to eat. It is a basic survival instinct steering every human being since the day they were born. When you fast, you make a conscious decision not to eat, provoking a profound psychological, emotional, and spiritual reaction from within. It will begin to uncover hidden fears, which often extend well beyond those relating to just food and the lack of it. The ego becomes painfully transparent while fasting, but it is this clarity that will help you see your opiate dependency as nothing more than an influential, petty dictator of your life. Habits and fears that caused you to fall into opiate addiction will begin to peel away. With time and experience, you will gain a mental and physical understanding, realizing that you will not die by temporarily denying yourself food for a little while. You will appreciate that the ego's desire for food and opiates is just that: a desire, and nothing more. You will begin to recognize all other desires of the ego as merely desires. Instead of your ego controlling you, you will start to control your ego. You will become empowered by acquiring the freedom to be, without the ego dominating your choices and behaviors.

As the ego releases its grip on you, emotional traumas from the past may resurface, although now you will experience them from a new perspective. When you let go of your ego, you also release the past and how it has been defining your present. You will start to be more grounded in the here and now, and in the freedom of the present moment. Your entire relationship with the world will begin to change once you are able to just be settled in the present moment. Love will start to blossom instead of fear dominating your life, naturally leading you to deeper states of consciousness, both within each fast and more gradually throughout your everyday life.

Water is an essential aspect to the existence of life on this planet. Without water, life would not exist or be able to survive. It acts as a perfect conductor of energy throughout our bodies and cells. Physics describes water as a perfect crystalline matrix, allowing information to be passed on coherently between cells. Under a microscope, this flux of energy is seen as a rainbow of vibrant colors.

Water has very unique characteristics. Not only does it have three forms, but there's actually a fourth form of water that has a similar consistency to honey. It is what causes your gelatin-like substances to have that texture. Oddly enough, on a molecular level water is actually a crystal and not a liquid. This unique characteristic allows for what is referred to as water structuring or structured water. Through recent experiments, scientists are able to store data or information on crystals due to its infinite storage capacity. Water has the ability to store information as well, because it is essentially a crystal. The terminology used to describe this is *Water Memory*.

In 2008, Masaru Emoto, a Japanese author and scientist, hypothesized that human consciousness affects the molecular structure of water. He discovered that water reacts to positive thoughts and words. From his observations, he found that polluted water could be cleaned through prayer and positive visualization. Emoto found that water is a "blueprint for our reality" and emotional energies and vibrations can change its physical structure.

Emoto's water crystal experiments consisted of exposing water in glasses to different words, pictures, and music. After freezing it, he then used microscopic photography to examine the aesthetic properties of resulting crystals. He learned that water exposed to positive speech and thoughts would result in visually pleasing crystals, whereas harmful intentions would yield ugly frozen crystal formations.

Dr. Emoto also showed that different water sources would produce different crystalline structures. For example, a water sample collected from a mountain stream, when frozen, would show structures of beautifully shaped crystal designs, resembling tiny geometric snowflakes. A sample taken from a polluted water source would reveal distorted and randomly formed crystalline structures. As soon as the dirty water was exposed to ultraviolet light or electromagnetic waves, a beautiful crystalline structure would then appear.

Water is significant to all living things and without it living organisms could not survive. In some organisms, up to 90% of their body weight comes from water. Up to 60% of the human adult body is water. According to H.H. Mitchell, Journal of Biological Chemistry, the brain and heart are composed of 73% water, and the lungs are about 83% water. The skin contains 64% water, muscles and kidneys are 79%, and even the bones are watery at 31%. The water in our body is continuously affected by positive and negative thoughts, actions, and words, as well as everything you listen to and surround yourself with. Water is the source of life for every living organism on this planet. We cannot live without it because it creates coherency within our bodies and allows our cells and internal organs to function properly.

During a 24-hour pure water fast, your body will begin searching for energy produced by food. When this energy is not found, it will start gathering energy from accumulated toxic sources. As toxins are internally eliminated from your body, opiate withdrawal symptoms will become less prevalent, making it easier for you get through the 24-hour time period required before you can begin taking your medication.

You can start a 24-hour water fast two hours after your last solid meal. Drink 8 oz. of pure filtered water every hour for the first 8 hours, dropping it down to 8 oz of water every 2 hours, until reaching your 24-hour time limit. When reintroducing your body to food, following your fast, start off slow and light with foods like fresh fruit, cottage cheese, yogurt, and plain oatmeal. Putting small portions of organic food back into your body gradually throughout the day will give you clarity and stamina. By the next day, you should be able to stomach a normal, solid meal.

Fasting may seem difficult for you at first because you are conditioned to believe that lack of food is unhealthy. Your body responds to this form of conditioning by growling at you when its hungry! They are just hunger pains; they will not kill you. What they will do is benefit your health in ways you cannot imagine, diminishing your body of toxins and diseases while paving the way to a successful recovery.

CHAPTER X

Ascended Masters and Spirit Guides

"That which you see through the raised consciousness is the image of the Master Kuthumi who is an infinite being of Wisdom and Love. He has a strong association with the Master Jesus and His teachings, endearing this Master to those who keep faith in the Christ. His help with those of you working on self-awareness is intense and He bestows special energies in this area. Many of Earth's mysteries which have long been a source of curiosity to Humankind will be clarified through this master's Spiritual manifestation. Such activities are due in part to the shift in mass consciousness which also has its effect on life universally. His love enfolds you."

—*Unknown*

MEETING YOUR SPIRIT GUIDE MEDITATION

Breath in and out three times slowly and deeply. On your third deep exhale, imagine your heart center located in the middle of your chest. Visualize your heart beating. Try to hear your heart beating as a sound, now feel it as a vibration. Focus on the sensation your heart creates as it pumps blood and oxygen through out your body. After focusing your awareness on the beating of your heart as a sensation, use intention to send the beating sensation from your heart to your hands. Now send it to your fingertips. Can you feel that? You just diverted blood to your fingertips simply by thinking about it. This is the quickest way to get rid of a migraine headache.

Now that you are aware of your inner power of intention, put your focus back on your heart beating in the center of your chest. Take three more long deep breaths in through your nose and out through your mouth. As you start to relax, imagine your heart center as a beautiful, white flower. Imagine the petals opening and closing with each beat of your heart. Now imagine a round, white, ball of photonic light in the center of the flower. See the light and feel its warmth and familiarity. When you are ready, imagine yourself entering the light. This is the porthole to your soul or inner self.

When you arrive, visualize yourself above the clouds in the heavenly realm of collected consciousness. Look up and see a magnificent temple stretching up as far as your eyes can see. Observe your heavenly temple carefully. Notice what it is made of, what color it is, and what kind of entrance awaits you at its heavenly gates. See yourself walking up a set of stairs leading to two large doors. Turn to your right and imagine seeing your spirit guide walking out of fog-like clouds, lovingly approaching and greeting you. Feel the deep love emitting from their heart chakra to yours. As they reach for your hand, graciously accept their loving gesture, and ask them their name. Write down the first word that comes to mind. Study their face looking deep into their eyes. Notice what they look like and what they are wearing. Thank them for always looking after you, especially times you felt especially lost and alone. They have always remained by your side. Thank them for giving you the opportunity to know them on a personal level and for giving you the strength to fight your inner demons. Now say goodbye and promise that from now on you will call upon them by name when you need their loving guidance and direction. Take three more long deep breaths and try to feel your heart beating once more as a sensation, as a sound, as a vibrational energy frequency. See in your mind's eye, your heart vibrantly beating in the center of your chest. Envision a round orb of white bio-photonic light growing larger and closer with each heartbeat. Take three more long deep breaths. Enter the light and come back into your body and into reality. Namaste.

Write down whatever word came to mind when you asked your Spirit Guide their name. Address them by this name whenever you call upon them for help. This heavenly being was personally appointed to you before you were born, and has remained by your side, protecting and guiding you through your past and present lives. Their mission is to make sure you reach your soul's true purpose, which will in turn lead to the benefit of all humanity.

Every living organism on this planet, including humans, are made up of conscious collective energy. Attention that is focused on that energy while at the same time experiencing conscious thought and deep, heartfelt emotion, activates the power of manifestation. Psychological and emotional stability is fundamentally coherent with your physical body. Mental conditioning from past experiences dictates the status of your growth and healing as well as your physical decomposition. When you experience positive thoughts and emotions, the energy produced unites with the infinite sea of universal collective consciousness, becoming a singular perspective. The moment you intensely focus your attention enough on specific thoughts and emotions, thought form is created. Clearly visualizing your needs and desires while experiencing the feelings as if they have already come into fruition will quickly transform thought-form into physical conscious reality.

Practicing manifestation is merely utilizing your inherited capability to co-create. The Bible tells us that God created us in his image and manifested the entire Universe and everything in it using this same fundamental field of conscious energy and awareness. He graciously gave each one of us the same ability to create, using physical thoughts and emotions as tools.

After death, our conscious soul leaves this earthly dimension. The energy flowing through our material body dissipates and is quickly absorbed by Source energy, returning to where it originated, in the infinite sea of universal collective consciousness. Your soul stays there until it is prepared to reincarnate back onto Earth. Before your soul enters another physical body at the time of re-birth, it must first meet with the Great White Brotherhood in the spirit realm. This is when your next life lessons and soul purpose will be carefully chosen and reviewed by you and the Ascended Masters.

Ascended Masters are all members of the Great White Brotherhood. The term "white" refers to the aura of white light that surrounds them. The Brotherhood works with earnest seekers and public servants of every race, religion, and walk of life to assist humans in the greater good for the evolution of our planet. These masters are teachers of mankind. They teach the path of overcoming adversity whereby the soul can reunite with the Higher Self, walking the Earth with self-mastery, following in the footsteps of Jesus Christ. When they complete the earthly tasks for which they were sent and devote a lifetime of sacred service, they will return to the heavenly realm becoming Ascended Masters, Spirit Guides, and Archangels.

Many of these ascended spiritual beings are familiar to us because at one time they walked the Earth as humans. During their material existence on Earth they proved themselves victorious over sin, disease, death, and every other human conflict, allowing them to transcend to higher levels of consciousness in the spirit realm. The Ascended Masters are directly associated with our personal assistance, growth, and ascension. Their Divine energy is constantly fueled by our positive conscious awareness aiming towards benefiting the greater good of mankind. As conscious energy is collected, these ascended spiritual beings take on the appearance of pure bio-photonic light. Divine Source uses these specific spiritual thought forms because of the conscious connection humans share with them, generating through the same light energy.

Ascended Masters, Spirit Guides and Archangels have balanced what the East refers to as karma and the West refers to as sin. They have transmuted all energies they utilized on the earth plane and returned to the core existence of "I AM THAT I AM."

It is written, "And a cloud received him out of their sight." This cloud is a field of electronic or spiritual energy called the Divine Monad. It is the I AM Presence that appeared to Moses as the flame burning in the bush. This Presence is our origin, our True Being, by way of which we too can attain cosmic consciousness. Our own God-source is ever-present within and above us, hovering like a cloud of infinite spiritual energy. Every master in Heaven has already merged with the Spirit of the I AM Presence. By proving the laws of God, the masters demonstrate that every human has the potential to obtain immortality through positive conscious thoughts, words, and actions.

The Ascended Masters teach by example, without words or platitudes, revealing to us the next step of our spiritual evolution. The Masters have experienced life in the physical plane at one time, making them well-qualified guides to show us the correct life path. Although they are mankind's most powerful spiritual teachers, they are also still students who are always learning new ways to assist and benefit mankind.

Every Ascended Master is unique in the cosmic sense of the word, having a specific person or persons on the earth plane that they are appointed to help bless, heal, and teach. When you accomplish your true soul purpose and balance your karma, you will have brought forth constructive good to the Earth and to mankind, proving that you are an asset to the positive evolution of our planet. The Ascended Masters are always there waiting for you to address their presence and ask for spiritual assistance in reaching heightened conscious awareness and spiritual goals.

Opiate addiction is part of the degradation of mankind and the deterioration of our beautiful planet. Calling upon your Spirit Guide and Ascended Masters for help and guidance in overcoming your addiction to opiates will benefit mankind by saving a life and getting one step closer to creating a peaceful world void of misery. Your Ascended Masters and Spirit Guide are just waiting for you to make the call so that they can grant you whatever you need in order to reach your soul's highest potential on Earth.

Calling on your Ascended Masters and spirit-guides is simple. Just close your eyes and relax your body by inhaling and exhaling three times slowly and deeply. Now repeat three times aloud:

"I call upon my Ascended Masters and Spirit Guide (name of Spirit Guide) to please assist me in (your earnest most heartfelt desire.)" After you repeat your affirmations asking them for help, lovingly thank them and end your session with the words: "So mote it be." It is really that simple! Very quickly, you will begin to experience changes guiding you to spiritual growth and evolution and making it possible for you to combat Opiate Use Disorder.

CHAPTER XI

Vibrational Frequencies

"It is the enigmas, the mysteries, and paradoxes that take hold of the imagination, leading it on the most exquisite dance."
—*Mae Won Hoe, Biochemist, Geneticist, and Author*

Frequency and vibration hold a significant hidden power that effects your life, your mental and physical health, and your consciousness. The science of cymatics, which is the study of visible sound and vibration, proves that vibration and frequency are the organizational foundation for the creation of all matter and life. When sound waves move through a physical medium such as land or water, the frequency of the waves has a direct effect upon the structures. This works within the human body as well.

One of the most common frequencies often talked about is the frequency of 432 HZ. Hertz refers to the number of vibrations or cycles per second. This specific frequency is essential because it vibrates on the principal of

Golden Ratio Phi, and unifies the properties of space, time, light, gravity, matter, and magnetism, using biology, DNA code, and consciousness. It has profound

effects on the cellular levels of the human body, as well as on expanding consciousness, and is considered a superior tuning due to its positive impact on overall health and wellbeing.

Every particle that exists in the Universe is in a constant state of vibration. This includes all matter, humans, and the Earth itself. Every cell and organ in your body carries its own vibrational frequency. Modern scientific research shows that each cell resonates with and responds to certain frequencies. When you are in resonance or the act of resonating and producing positive emotions, you are in balance. Music played at 432 HZ, creates a vibration inside the human body, while at the same time balancing the mental and emotional state. It transmits beneficial healing energy because it is considered a pure tone of math fundamental to nature.

Our current musical standard is a tuning of 440 HZ, which came into effect when the International Standards Organization (ISO) endorsed it in 1953. There is a theory that the change from 432 HZ to 440 HZ came about because of the recommendations from the Nazi party spokesperson, Yosef Goebbels, in 1939. According to this theory, there was an organized effort to change concert pitch, at the start of the 20th century, to codify an old-world New Order of central pitch. This developed to increase levels of anxiety in individuals, causing them to think and feel in specific ways, and making them prisoners in a consciousness that produces disharmony. It is also alleged that the Rockefeller Foundation had an interest in making sure the United States adopted the 440 HZ standard as part of a war on consciousness, causing more emotional distress, and in turn, more physical illness and hardship. Whether these theories are true or not, one thing is sure. The frequency that music is tuned to has a profound effect on humans. This is not just a spiritual concept, but has been both mathematically and scientifically proven. Nikola Tesla stated, "If we can control that resonate system electronically, we can directly control the entire mental system of humankind."

Resonance sound healing dates back to the earliest records of human civilization. Ancient Egyptians clearly understood the scientific technology behind sound waves, and how they are used to balance and heal the body. Ancient Egyptians believed that at the beginning of creation, Thoth, the eldest son of Ra, cracked open the world egg, and with the sound of his voice, began the creation process. Thoth was considered the most powerful friend of the soul, and with the trueness and purity of his voice, made the resurrection of the human soul possible. Egyptians considered sound frequencies fundamentally crucial to their existence. They believed sacred sound was the single element directly connecting them to the Divine, who possessed the power and authority to grant them the gift of immortality. This was only possible if their physical vibrations were in harmony with the energy frequencies the Earth was emitting.

The ancient Hymns of Hermes states that: "the sacred sounds pour forth blessings, and open a path throughout nature, straight to the Divine." All ancient Vedic texts from India, dating back 5,000 years or more, teach that the use of sacred sound was the fastest way humans could reach spiritual awakening and enlightenment. They believed that with the continuous singing of harmonious chants, they would eventually gain immortality and become one with the gods.

The ancient Egyptian deity Ra does not only personify the sun but also symbolizes the brilliant energy of light that it provides, making the existence of life on Earth possible. Isis, the ancient Egyptian goddess, and queen of heaven, received the secret name of Ra. She tricked it out of him when he was on his death bed after being bitten by a venomous snake. She could do anything once she had access to his secret name because it held the sound codes of creation. The ancient account, found in The Egyptian Book of the Dead, reads: "She uttered the spell with the magical power of her mouth. Her tongue was perfect, and it never halted at a word. Beneficent in command, and word, was Isis, the woman of magical spells. On the bark of the sun, the swallow is the first to announce the return of the light, singing the dawn of a new day. In the dark marrow of my bones, I have made myself light. I am the swallow, spinning at the start, through whom light enters the sky, who flies formless, above a world of forms, ringing across the horizon. "Enter me! I shall make you a god!" she cried. Enchantress, and wife, she stamps, and spins. She raises her arms to dance, and from her armpits rises a hot perfume that fills the sails of boats along the Nile. She stirs the breezes that make the sailors swoon. Under her spell, I come to myself, under her body, I come to life. She dances and draws down heaven. As above, so below."

The dominant notes in a swallow's natural tone, when measured with a bio acoustic sampling machine, is C and F sharp, which ironically are the same frequencies emanating as elements and color from one of the most massive stars in our galaxy. Egyptian manuscripts have shown that Egyptians used musical notation with seven related tones and seven associated colors. Their harps were constructed with strings matching the colors of the rainbow. These same seven tones and colors also represent the seven chakras, which are part of the human energy system.

Egyptian temples are built in alignment with the heavens, and each temple is tuned to a different musical scale based on its dimensions and proportions. Music was used to regulate both the material and immaterial worlds for ancient Egyptians. They believed that a string resonates with the macrocosm of the Universe and the microcosm of the human soul. The Hymns of Hermes states that: "the order of singers maintained the harmonious patterns, enchanting earth, and sky." In the manuscript called The Key, Hermes teaches the way to enlightenment by chanting hymns of praise and pouring these blessings out onto all beings. He also used sacred words of power to raise the inner resonance and become a god. Temple singers used specific tones to create healing in the body, mind, and soul.

Your own voice can also work as an instrument for healing, connecting you with universal magnetic energy frequencies. It can reveal where you currently are in the physical, emotional, and spiritual evolution of things, and explain what you can do to become a fully enlightened spiritual being. Ancient traditions, seen all over the world, can help you to open our heart and connect with higher levels of consciousness and more enormous potentialities.

The resonance of sound healing has an untold history. Apollo was the ancient Greek god who personified music and medicine. Aesculapius was able to cure mental disorders with songs. The well-known philosophers Plato and Aristotle claimed that music affected the soul and human emotions. During Biblical times, instruments became used to defeat evil spirits from human souls, while many Native American cultures use song and dance to heal the sick.

Fast forward to the 1940s, when the United States military incorporated music into their programs. This was used for the recuperation of army personnel during World War II, often described as the dawn of musical therapy. Today, sound healing is used in many aspects of medicine and spiritual growth practices. While still considered an alternative to Western medicine, a mass of evidence suggests that it is useful and necessary for the emotional and psychological health of humans.

Sound healing therapy involves using music to improve the physical, psychological, emotional, and spiritual health of an individual. This type of treatment is known to improve many facets of a person's life, including emotional and social development, cognitive motor functioning, as well as psychological and psychiatric stability. There are several forms of sound therapy, which include listening or singing along with the music, improvising musical acts, meditating, chanting, and playing musical instruments. Some specialists subject the patient to individually crafted sounds to induce positive brainwaves.

Almost everything you experience in the Universe is based on your perception of energy waves. When waves of sound energy reach your ears, they are converted into electrical signals that travel up the auditory nerve, into the auditory cortex, and up into the brain. This is where all sounds are processed. Once they settle in the mind, specific responses are triggered in your body, altering your emotions, releasing hormones, and stimulating certain impulses.

In recent neurological studies, it was proven that the application of specific frequencies by frequency generating devices can enhance cellular resonance and cellular metabolic and electrical functions. It has recently been discovered that healthy human tissues have more structured water than unhealthy tissues. Clinicians who recognize this fact found that certain types of music, frequency generators, and chanting provide water structuring throughout the body when correctly utilized.

Pulsed Electro-Magnetic Field Therapy (PEMF) has become a popular method of treatment for a wide variety of physical ailments. This is a process that involves directing powerful pulsed energy waves towards damaged or injured areas of a patient's body. Although rarely talked about mainstream, NASA recognizes the benefits of this type of therapy as well. In a recent NASA paper entitled: "Physiological and Molecular Electro Magnetic Fields on Human Neuron Cells," written by Thomas J. Goodwin, Ph.D., he states that, "As is clearly demonstrated in the human body, the bioelectric, biochemical process of electrical nerve stimulation, is a documented reality. The present investigation demonstrates that a similar phenomenon can be potentiated in a synthetic atmosphere. One may use this potentiation for a number of purposes, which includes developing tissues for transplantation, repairing traumatized tissues, and moderating some neurodegenerative diseases, and perhaps controlling the degeneration of tissue."

Frequency has a hidden power, affecting your thoughts and your mind, as well as your entire body and, ultimately, society as a whole.

When music is based upon a tuning standard of your choosing, it can resonate with the earth's frequency and attune us to a consciousness that aligns with a positive life. Sound is more than just vibratory signals. It interacts with experience and helps shape and sustain it. It acts as a conduit of conscious intent between people, societies, and entire civilizations. Humans are all forms of energy bounded by frequency.

Listening to the right kind of music makes people more productive and creative. Sound healing can also relieve stress and improve negative moods and behaviors. This is true because listening to music floods your brain with the pleasure chemical dopamine, the same chemical released when you use opiates. Sounds also cause the release of a naturally produced pain killer called oxytocin. This hormone allows you to bond with others and is produced naturally by the body when a woman is experiencing labor and delivery. Sound healing is so powerful it can change your brain, which in turn affects your body. A 2008 study done by the Journal of Advanced Nursing discovered that those who listen to music feel less pain and experience less anxiety than those who do not.

All forms of sound resonate at different frequencies, and humans emit the same waves of energy as the earth in the form of electromagnetic energy waves. Harmonic resonance occurs when frequencies become lined up, forming balance with sounds that are conducive to healing and relaxation. A study conducted in the 1970s proposed that when one tone gets played in one ear, and a different tone gets played in the other, the right and left hemispheres of the brain connect. This creates a third internal tone, referred to as a binaural beat. These tones synchronize the brain, providing clarity, alertness, and higher concentration. This is evidence that your mind and body responds to sound positively, in both a cognitive and physical way.

Some forms of sound therapy are scientific, while others denote a spiritual nature. They each share the same common ground in which sounds are the basis of healing and development. One method is called the Banny Method, which involves not only sound, but guided imagery as well, and assists patients struggling with physiological, and psychological problems. Music and pictures are shown, which the patient is told to focus on before discussing the issues they are having. Another popular method of sound healing is known as Dalcroze Eurythmics, which is a technique used to teach music to students as a form of therapy. It focuses on rhythm and expression as a part of learning and development. This method of treatment increases awareness and significantly improves motor and cognitive functions in the brain.

Mantra-guided healing is practiced through the art of meditation. Your voice, thoughts, and emotions are instruments in their own right, and when they are used during meditation you are practicing a powerful form of individual sound healing therapy with yourself. As we have seen in previous chapters, meditation has many neurological and psychological benefits. Chanting, or repeating specific mantras or prayers during meditation, improves sleep patterns, lowers blood pressure, calms the mind, reduces stress, and improves mood, breathing, and circulation. Sound therapy is also successful in treating drug dependency and depression. The same applies to guided meditation, in which you meditate according to voiced instruction.

A well-intentioned song flows through your body, extending a natural vibration that connects you to every other living organism on Earth. An entanglement of positive bio photonic waves becomes evident, directly influencing the health and overall wellbeing of humans, plants, and animals. The internal voice or consciousness within each human creates the same frequency as external sound waves. Your thoughts are always directing your choices, judgments, and decisions, which are all based on past conditioning and how you view the world. You can learn to be consciously aware of your thoughts and vibrational frequencies using a simple tool called mindfulness. Practicing mindfulness will clear your mind of past negative mental and emotional conditioning, allowing you to have a positive outlook on the world and enabling you to manifest a positive world for yourself and the rest of humanity. When you become familiar with using positive affirmations regularly, a protective spiritual layer will form, guarding you against future negative vibrations. Once this happens, you will quickly begin to realize that you are the Universe, manifesting through a human nervous system and becoming self-aware.

Try for a moment to envision a fiery torch being spun around, creating the appearance of a burning circle. When held steady, the circle vanishes, vibrating or not. It is the same everywhere, at all times. Your words, thoughts, and actions create vibrational frequencies, constantly transmitting energy to the Universe. These can either make you feel completely fulfilled, or the exact opposite, entirely unfulfilled. The collective sea of universal consciousness gathers both positive and negative energy waves you are emitting. It is fundamentally important that you train yourself to become consciously aware of the vibrations you are sending out, every minute of every day.

Bio photonic energy waves flow through the body, beaming out all around you in the form of bio photons. These ultraviolet energy particles are blocked by negative social conditioning, which causes you to feel spiritually and emotionally imbalanced. It is just as easy to unblock these energy centers and restore balance and vitality. Similar to a technique used in ancient Egypt, a practice known as "chakra balancing," can restore and balance the primary energy centers in your body. This therapy practice combines sound healing vibrations with mental visualization, and is known to have a lasting, positive influence over the mind, body, and spirit.

When using sound resonance and mental visualization for chakra balancing, it is vital to familiarize yourself with each chakra's location in the body, its color, and it's associated internal organ. The different colors of the chakras are known to influence a person's health and emotions. For instance, if someone is having problems with their heart, and they bathe in green bathwater, it can help balance out inconsistencies involving that chakra. Receiving too much of the color green can cause the opposite effect. For example, if someone has their bedroom walls painted green, overstimulation of the heart chakra can occur, causing an imbalance, and resulting in other health complications.

Throughout history, several philosophies, mystic traditions, religions, and alternative medicine frameworks include the concept of chakras. By balancing them, you can become connected to overall health and the evolution of consciousness. The word "chakra" in Sanskrit means wheel, disc, or circle, which is the shape of its energy structure. Although chakras are commonly depicted as a circle, when observed through clairvoyance they are a cone with the tip close to the skin.

The chakra system, originated in India, between 1500 and 500 B.C., in the oldest text, known as the Vedas. These are the earliest Sanskrit literary records, and the most ancient scriptures of Hinduism. The seven chakras each correspond to specific organs, as well as physical, emotional, psychological, and spiritual states of being, and influence all areas of life. Within these chakras is *Prana*, or the ultimate pure healing energy surrounding us and keeping us happy, healthy, and vibrant. Chakras are real, but being able to detect the existence of chakras involves the ability to perceive your subtle energies, through a form of psychic ability. As it is the case of every human's capacity, you can learn to understand and work with your chakras. All it takes is a little bit of theory, technique, practice, and persistence.

The first, or "root" chakra is symbolized by a lotus flower, and signified by the color red. In Sanskrit, it is called *Muladhara*, which translates into "root, and basis of existence." This chakra is sturdy, stabilizing, and supportive, keeping everything connected, as long as its functioning correctly. Physically, it is associated with the base of the spine, the pelvic floor, and the first three vertebrae. It is responsible for an individual's sense of security and survival. It is also connected to whatever you use to ground yourself, including basic needs, such as food, water, shelter, and safety. This also includes your more emotional needs, such as letting go of fear and feeling safe. As you know, when these needs become met, worries seem to diminish naturally. When this chakra is blocked, a variety of physical ailments can occur, which include anxiety disorders, fears, or nightmares. Internally this chakra is associated with problems in the colon, bladder, with elimination, or with lower back, leg, or feet issues.

The second, or "sacral" chakra is associated with the color orange, and is seen as the element of water. It is called *Svadhisthana* in Sanskrit, which translates into "where your being is established." It is located above the pubic bone, below the navel, and is responsible for your sexual and creative energies. When this chakra is aligned, you will feel great, and your friendly, passionate, and successfully fulfilled nature will come out. It will also elicit feelings of wellness, abundance, pleasure, and joy. By honoring your body and expressing yourself creatively, you are keeping the energy wheels turning and fluid. When the sacral chakra is blocked, you will feel uninspired creatively, or experience some form of emotional instability. Imbalance of this chakra can also represent sexual disfunction, and potentially experiencing fear of change, depression, or addictive behaviors.

The third, or "solar plexus" chakra is associated with the color yellow, and is represented with fire and the power of transformation. It is called *Manipura* in Sanskrit, which translates into "resplendent gem," or "lustrous gem." It is the primary chakra, according to ancient Vedic tradition. This chakra is said to be your source of personal power, ruling over self-esteem. It is the action and balance which focuses on individual willpower, personal strength, and commitment. This chakra is located from the naval to about the ribcage. It governs all things metabolic, digestive, and stomach related. When this chakra is blocked, you can suffer from low self-esteem, have difficulty making important decisions, and may have anger or control issues. Blockages can also cause you to express apathy or procrastination publicly, or become easily taken advantage of. You are also likely to suffer from stomach issues of some kind, such as heartburn or indigestion.

As the central chakra, the fourth, or "heart" chakra is represented by the color green, and is associated with balance, calmness, and serenity. It is called *Anahata* in Sanskrit, which translates into "unhurt, unstuck, and unbeaten." This chakra, located at the center of your chest, is where the physical and spiritual meet. Physically it encapsulates the heart, the thymus gland (which plays a vital role in your endocrine and lymphatic system), the lungs, and the breasts. It is represented by love, spiritual awakening, forgiveness, and service. When your heart chakra is aligned and balanced, love and compassion are flowing freely, both in terms of giving and receiving. A closed heart chakra can give way to grief, anger, jealousy, fear of betrayal, and hatred toward yourself and others. This can especially be in the form of holding a grudge against something or someone.

The fifth, or "throat" chakra is represented by the color blue, and is located in the throat region, with its activation point situated in the pit of the throat. It is called *Vishuddha* in Sanskrit, which translates into "especially pure." This chakra is all about expressing your inner truth, or, specifically, ensuring that your hidden truths get adequately communicated. The throat chakra rules all communication and is the first of the three spiritual chakras (as opposed to the lower ones which manifest themselves more physically). Anatomically, this chakra is associated with the thyroid, parathyroid, jaw, neck, mouth, tongue, and larynx. When this chakra is in proper balance, you can fully listen, as well as speak and express yourself clearly with others. When this chakra is blocked, in addition to having trouble speaking your truth, you find it difficult to pay attention and stay focused. You may also experience fear of judgment from others, which can further hinder your ability to express yourself openly. Physically, this blockage can manifest itself as a sore throat, thyroid issues, neck, and shoulder stiffness, or tension headaches.

The color purple or violet represents the sixth, or "third eye" chakra. It is called *Ajna* in Sanskrit, which translates into "guru chakra," or "third-eye chakra." This chakra is located directly between your eyebrows, and represents the pituitary gland, eyes, head, and lower part of the brain, all governed by the third eye, which Western science recognizes as resting in the pineal gland. This area reportedly governs your intuition and can recognize and tap into it. It is responsible for all things between you and the outside world and serves as a bridge between the two. It allows you to cut through any illusions and drama and see things more clearly. When this chakra becomes blocked, you may have trouble accessing your intuition, trusting your inner voice, recalling essential facts, or learning new skills. If your lower chakras - the root, sacral, solar plexus, and heart - are unbalanced, your third eye will likely be as well. This will cause you to act more judgmental, dismissive, and introverted. A third eye blockage is associated with a broad range of issues including depression, anxiety, and addiction. Physically, the blockage of this chakra causes headaches, dizziness, and several other health issues involving the brain.

The seventh, or "crown" chakra is represented by the colors white and gold, is considered the center of enlightenment, and is your spiritual connection to your higher self, others, and the Divine. It is called *Sahasrara* in Sanskrit, which translates into "thousand-petaled."

This chakra is described as a lotus flower with a thousand petals of different colors. These petals become arranged in twenty layers, each layer with approximately fifty petals. The pericarp is golden, and within it a circular moon region is inscribed, with a luminous triangle that can be either upward or downward pointing. This chakra is located at the top of your head. When aligned, it can bring about realizations that occur when you are along the lines of pure awareness and complete consciousness. Undivided and all-expansive, it is said to be more significant than you, part of one giant Universe. A crown chakra blockage may create feelings of isolation or emotional distress, making you feel disconnected from everyone and everything. You might feel like your usual self, just not in an elevated state of spiritual connection and enlightenment. Unlike the other chakras, the crown chakra is typically only opened up fully through specific yogic or meditative exercises. Anything from meditation, prayer, to moments of silent gratitude can create a spiritual connection, keeping the crown chakra in proper balance.

A mantra is a sound, syllable, word, or group of words that is considered capable of "creating transformation." The Sanskrit word "mantra" consists of the root "man" which translates in English "to think", and the suffix "tra" translates into "tools or instruments," hence a literal translation would be "instrument of thought." A *Bija* mantra – *Bija* meaning "seed" - is a one-syllable "seed sound" that when said aloud activates the energy of the chakras. These specific sounds are used to purify and balance the mind and body. When you speak the *Bija* mantras, you resonate with the energy of the associated chakra, helping you focus upon your intuitive awareness of your body and its needs.

Chant the *Bija* mantras, either one at a time or in sequences, as repetition can help you access a meditative state.

You can balance your chakras yourself, by using the sound of your voice or even your thoughts to create a natural energy vibration while practicing mental visualization. All you need is a peaceful, quiet place, where you will not be disturbed for about 20 to 30 minutes; a conscious mind; and an inner or outer voice. With these tools, you will be able to utilize ancient techniques which will very quickly begin the healing process and guide you down the path to a successful recovery. It is quick, easy, and free, and you will start to notice results instantly.

After you find a quiet, comfortable spot, you can sit in a chair, with your spine straight and your hands gently placed on your lap, palms facing upward. Or, position yourself lying flat on your back, with your arms at your side, palms facing upward. Whatever position is more comfortable for you, as long as the base of your spine is positioned in a straight line with the crown of your head.

Once correctly positioned, close your eyes and begin to become aware of your breathing. Breathe slowly and deeply, in through your nose and out through your mouth. Sometimes it helps to count four seconds on the inhale, hold your breath for four seconds, and then count five seconds on the exhale. You want your stomach to be rising with each inhale, not your chest. It might take a little practice, but you will get the hang of it. As you breathe, you will begin to feel extremely relaxed and centered. On your third exhale, imagine a small, round, red vortex of light spinning around your root chakra at the base of your spine, clearing out any blockages. As you envision this spinning ball of red light, slowly utter the sound "YAM" (pronounced YOM). Allow the mantra to flow out of your mouth with each deep exhale, three or four times. You have just successfully balanced your root chakra.

Now imagine an orange ball of light, spinning in, out, and around the physical area of your sacral chakra, which is your pelvic area located beneath your belly button. Imagine this orange vortex of light energy clearing away any blockages, restoring your sacral chakra to its original balanced state. Continue to inhale and exhale slowly and deeply, and on your exhale, utter the sound "VAM" (pronounced VOM).

Now, move on to your solar plexus chakra. As you continue inhaling and exhaling slowly and deeply, imagine a yellow ball of light, spinning in, out, and around your solar plexus chakra. This is located just above your belly button in your abdominal region. As you imagine this yellow vortex of light energy clearing any blockages and returning your third chakra to a balanced state, on your exhale, slowly utter the sound "RAM" (pronounced ROM).

As you continue to breathe in and out slowly and deeply, imagine a green ball of energy spinning around the center of your chest at your heart, which is the location of your heart chakra. Imagine a green vortex of light energy clearing away any blockages, and slowly utter the sound "YAM" (pronounced YOM) as you exhale.

Next, as you continue to breathe, envision a blue ball of light spinning in, out, and around the location of your throat chakra, located in the center of your throat. As you imagine this blue vortex of light energy clearing away any blockages, on your exhale, slowly utter the sound "HAM" (pronounced HOM).

As you continue breathing in and out slowly and deeply, imagine a violet or light purple colored ball of light spinning in, out, and around the location of your third eye chakra, located directly between your eyebrows. As you imagine this violet vortex of light energy clearing away any blockages, slowly utter the sound "OM" (pronounced with a long O).

Finally, continue inhaling and exhaling slowly and deeply. At the same time, imagine a gold or white ball of light spinning around the top of your head. Imagine this golden or white vortex of light energy clearing away any blockages from your crown chakra, and once again slowly utter the sound, "OM" (pronounced with a long O).

You have just successfully cleared away blockages from the primary energy centers in your body, restoring them to balance. Clearing your chakras will help you successfully find lasting recovery by bringing you back to a level of conscious awareness. Now you will begin feeling energized and start to experience lasting fulfillment in your life. Congratulations! You just got one step closer to your recovery goals! I am so proud of you!

CHAPTER XII

30-Day Path to Freedom + Personal Progress Calendar

"Letting go gives us freedom, and freedom is the only condition for happiness. If, in our heart, we still cling to anything – anger, anxiety, or possessions – we cannot be free."

—*Thich Nhat Hanh*

A great myriad of important information has been learned associated with the origin of opium, the roots of addiction, and the effects opioids have on your brain and body. You have also been shown how your thoughts and words, both positive and negative, create a vibrational frequency, and dictate the outcome of future events in your life. When lined up with the vibrational frequency of the cosmos, they are returned to you and create your reality. Positive words and thoughts create higher vibrations naturally in tune with the Universe. In contrast, negative words and thoughts create unfavorable results when a quantum connection forms between the two, proving that you truly are a co-creator of your own destiny.

Becoming consciously aware of messages transmitted to the Universe will not only help your material world but will have a lasting effect on your body and internal organs. This can either support good health or cause massive dysfunction in your body. Surrounding yourself with negative vibrational energy has proven to cause structural and developmental damage to cells and internal organs, creating illnesses and diseases. With your busy lifestyle and thousands of words and thoughts influencing your life each day, it is not surprising how difficult it can be to train your brain to become unambiguous to negativity. Recent studies have shown the possible adverse health consequences that can arise from harmful behaviors and thinking patterns. Negative attitudes and feelings of hopelessness can create chronic stress - upsetting the body's hormonal balance, depleting brain chemicals required for happiness, and damaging the immune system. Scientists have recently found that chronic stress can decrease our lifespan by shortening our telomeres. These are the "end caps" of our DNA strands, which cause us to age more quickly.

Poorly managed or repressed anger and hostility is also related to other health conditions, such as hypertension, high blood pressure, cardiovascular disease, digestive disorders, and various kinds of infections. Scientist Barbara Fredrickson has devoted over twenty years to researching and publishing the physical and emotional benefits of positivity. These include faster recovery from cardiovascular stress, better sleep, fewer colds, and a greater sense of overall happiness. Positive attitudes, such as playfulness, gratitude, awe, love, interest, serenity, and feeling connected to others have a direct impact on health and wellbeing, and we can easily learn to develop them ourselves with practice.

Too much time gets spent pondering over the minor frustrations you experience, such as bad traffic or a disagreement with a loved one. You usually ignore the opportunities that come your way to experience wonder, awe, and gratitude throughout the day. To offset this negativity bias and experience a harmonious emotional state of mind, Fredrickson proposes you need to experience three positive emotions for every negative one. This works intentionally for those who have a more pessimistic outlook on life.

Practicing forgiveness is another simple tool that will allow you to experience better mental, emotional, and physical health. Forgiveness means fully accepting that an adverse event has occurred, and relinquishing your negative feelings surrounding the circumstance. Forgiveness is a learned trait, as proven when the Stanford Forgiveness Project trained 260 adults on how to practice forgiveness in a unique six-week course. 70% reported a decrease in their feelings of hurt, 13% experienced reduced anger, and 27% experienced fewer physical complaints. The practice of forgiveness is also linked to better immune function and a longer lifespan. Other recent studies have shown that forgiveness has more than just a metaphorical effect on the heart. It can lower blood pressure and improve cardiovascular health as well.

Joy and gratitude, acknowledging the ethical aspects of life, and giving thanks also have a powerful impact on emotional wellbeing. In a landmark study, people who were asked to count their blessings felt happier. They also had more physical stamina, exercised more, had fewer physical complaints, and slept better than those who created lists of hassles. There is a relationship between joy and gratitude, but with a surprising twist: it is not joy that makes us grateful, but gratefulness that makes us joyful.

You may think that a disease or illness is the reason your body is always tired, and you often experience prolonged aches and pains. Have you ever considered that negativity could have something to do with it? Pessimism affects more than just your emotional health. Doctors have recently found that people with elevated levels of negativity-associated stress are more likely to suffer from degenerative brain disorders. They also recover from sickness much slower than those who have a positive mindset.

Negativity is often associated with feelings of depression or insecurity. It can stem from illness, life events, personality problems, and substance abuse. Like many things in life, negativity, too, can become habit-forming. Frequent criticism, cynical thoughts, and denial create neural pathways in the brain that encourage sadness. These negative tendencies can cause your mind to distort the truth, making it even more challenging to break the negative cycle. Experts say it takes at least 21 days to break a habit. Extended periods of negativity slow digestion and decreases the immune system's ability to fight inflammation. Therefore, negative people are more likely to get sick than optimists.

In the same way negative thoughts create neural pathways in the brain, positive self-talk and reinforcement can also become a habit. Researchers suggest that happiness and optimism are more of a choice, influenced by circumstance. If you want to overcome negative habits and thinking, learn to recognize what is real. See both the good and the bad in the world. The more you become a realistic optimist, the more you will be able to focus your energy on the positive. Live in the moment by focusing on the task at hand, and avoiding thinking of past mistakes or future fears. If you catch yourself having a negative thought or emotion, stop yourself and try reciting at least three positive affirmations at once. Positive thinkers learn to control their minds and are aware of the thoughts entering their heads. If being positive is a habit, then you need to practice optimism every day! Participate in activities that create happy thoughts, like hobbies, spending time with loved ones, mindfulness, and meditation. Media and people can have a detrimental influence on your negativity level, so you should always try to engage in uplifting media and positive conversations.

Experiencing negative thoughts and emotions is inevitable, but positive thinkers know how to turn them into action. For example, a positive thinker may look at herself in the mirror and notice that she has gained weight. Instead of dwelling on her appearance, she uses it as motivation to live a healthier lifestyle. Negativity is contagious, so do not catch the pessimist bug from someone. Instead, spend time talking with people who genuinely care about you and leave you feeling enlightened and content. Humans are social creatures, and developing a strong network of family and friends can help you see the glass as half full instead of half empty.

Mindful medically assisted treatment is fundamental for achieving successful recovery from opiate dependency. This practice involves taking your medication (preferably Suboxone or Zubsolv) at a specific time each day, and combining it with a daily mindful meditation practice. This will help repair neural pathways in your brain temporarily damaged due to prolonged opiate abuse. It will also help erase any negative conditioning or trauma you have experienced throughout your life still affecting you on a subconscious level. Negative conditioning and post-traumatic experiences are the core reasons you chose to turn to opiates in the first place.

Most mindfulness practices involve a person focusing their attention on one thought and one thought alone. An overarching goal is to become firmly affixed on the present moment. What this typically involves is focusing your attention on your breathing, and observing each inhalation and exhalation without consideration to other thoughts. The moment a stray thought arises, be quick to recognize it and then turn your attention back to focusing. Use your breathing and a mantra to help keep you focused.

If you have ever tried this before, you know how unbelievably difficult it can be, particularly when your attention span is taxed to the limit. Our minds are known for wandering, and moving from one thought to the next, especially if you are struggling with an addiction. It is hard enough just living your regular busy schedule to focus your attention on one specific thing; a daily mindfulness and meditation practice will help you with this.

The medial prefrontal cortex is an area in the brain sometimes referred to as the "Me Center". This part of the brain processes information relating to ourselves and our experiences, both past and present. Usually, the neural pathways from bodily sensation and fear centers of the brain to the "Me Center" are powerful. This is also where triggers take place that make you want to use opiates again. When you experience a scary or upsetting sensation, it triggers a strong reaction to your "Me Center," making you feel scared and under attack. When you meditate, you weaken this neural connection. What this means is that you will not react as strongly to sensations that might have once activated your medial prefrontal cortex. As you weaken the connection between the part of your brain known for reasoning and these fear centers, you can handle scary or upsetting feelings more rationally.

Recently neuroscientists have figured out a way to peer directly into the brain and discover what is happening, with the advent of MRI's and other brain scanning techniques paving the way. For example, neuroscientists observing MRI scans have found that meditation strengthens the brain by reinforcing the connections between brain cells. A 2012 study showed that people who meditate exhibit higher levels of gyrification — the "folding" of the cerebral cortex as a result of growth, which in turn may allow the brain to process information faster. Scientists suspect that gyrification is responsible for making the brain better at processing information, making decisions, forming memories, and improving attention.

Much of this research shows that meditation causes the brain to undergo physical changes, many of which are beneficial. Meditation is linked to cortical thickness, which can result in decreased sensitivity to pain. In 2009 there was a study conducted with the descriptive title, "Long-Term Meditation is Associated with Increased Gray Matter Density in the Brain Stem." MRIs were used to compare the brains of meditators with non-meditators. The structural differences observed led to the speculation that certain benefits, like improved cognitive, emotional, and immune responses, can be tied to this growth and its positive effects on breathing and heart rate.

The integrity of gray matter, which is a significant player in the central nervous system, is directly affected by opiate use. Meditation has been linked to larger hippocampus and frontal volumes of gray matter. After practicing a regular daily meditation practice, the results were more positive emotions, the retention of emotional stability, and more mindful behavior, including heightened focus during day-to-day living. Meditation has also shown to have neuron-protective attributes; and can diminish age-related effects on gray matter and reduce cognitive decline.

A study from earlier this year showed that meditators have a different expression of brain metabolites; specifically, metabolites linked to anxiety and depression. But it is not just the physical and chemical components of the brain that are affected by meditation. Neuroscientists have documented the way it impacts brain activity itself. For example, meditation has been associated with decreased activity in default mode network activity and connectivity — those undesirable brain functions responsible for lapses of attention, and disorders such as addiction, anxiety, ADHD, and the buildup of beta-amyloid plaques in Alzheimer's disease. And finally, meditation has been linked to dramatic changes in electrical brain activity - namely increased Theta and Alpha EEG activity, which is associated with wakeful and relaxed attention and opiate addiction.

Perhaps the most significant benefit of meditation is its ability to improve attention. In 2010, researchers looked at participants who practiced focused-attention meditation for about five hours each day, over three months. After conducting concentration tests, the participants proved they had an easier time sustaining voluntary attention. If you can concentrate for extended periods during meditation, it should carry over into your daily life. Focused attention is very much like a muscle, that needs to become strengthened through exercise. Five hours of meditation per day is a bit excessive; however, other studies show that 20 minutes a day is all that is required to receive beneficial results, like stress reduction and recovery from addiction.

Visualization techniques have been used by successful people to manifest successful outcomes for centuries. This practice has given many high achievers what appears to be super-powers. It enables them to create their dream life by accomplishing one goal at a time, with intense mental focus and confidence supporting them. We all possess this fantastic ability, though most of us have not been taught how to use it effectively. Elite athletes, extremely wealthy individuals, and peak performers have used the power of visualization to achieve greatness. The daily practice of visualizing your dreams as already complete can rapidly accelerate your achievement of those dreams, goals, and aspirations.

The following mindfulness exercises will allow you to rediscover yourself and reconnect consciously, enabling you to reap the benefits from the Universe that you are well deserving of. These exercises were created to help you clear away the wreckage from the past and erase mental conditioning that has been affecting you since the time you were born. Practicing them will strengthen your ability to continue moving forward and creating the life you have always wanted. It is best to do these exercises first thing in the morning, right after you wake up, or just before you go to sleep at night. The first thoughts and experiences you have upon waking will dictate the rest of your day. Whatever you think about right before falling asleep influences your subconscious mind and your life. Use the calendar provided, following each exercise to mark your recovery success. Wishing you the absolute best of luck on your journey to lasting and successful recovery.

SEA SALT CLEANSING BATH

A spiritual cleansing bath is a wonderful way to erase negative energy build-up, or simply ease a stressful day and refresh your energy field. An aura is the energy field that surrounds your physical body. It carries the vibrations of your thoughts, feelings, and beliefs. Your aura will mirror your physical world and vice versa. You might need a spiritual cleansing if you are:

Lethargic and unrested

Moody or overly emotional

Off-kilter and ungrounded

Cloudy, out of your head or unable to focus

Detoxing from opiates

You are constantly accumulating stray energy from anything or anyone you come into direct contact with throughout your day. Negative thoughts and emotions float through the atmosphere like particles of dust through a beam of light shining through a hole in the roof. This energetic debris is a natural byproduct of daily living. Our thoughts and emotions are vibrational electromagnetic energy fields that need a place to dissipate.

You will be especially vulnerable to energetic intrusion if you are sensitive, prone to depression or addiction, or display empathic tendencies. Cleansing your mind, body, and soul of the negative energy you have accumulated throughout your day is important for your well-being. Without the release of negative energy, you create more energetic blocks in your life that will manifest in the form of obstacles, illness, and disease.

Sea salt has been used for thousands of years for spiritual cleansing. It carries a detoxifying quality, drawing out any impurities and preparing your mind, body, and soul for the journey that lies ahead. Doing a Himalayan sea salt cleansing bath before you begin your regimen will allow you to start off on a clean slate, clearing away any negative occurrences happening in your life up until now.

Both water and salt have long been revered as energetically cleansing substances. Water is easily "programmed," and can hold onto the vibrations created by both your positive and negative thoughts, as well as your emotions. It can absorb and hold energy very easily and effectively. When we use water with the intention of cleansing our auras by sweeping away negative energy and debris, it will help absorb negative energy, removing it from our energy field.

Pink Himalayan sea salt works to further cleanse you of any negative energies. Salt is a natural collector of negative ions so it can collect negative energy from your home and your body. Also known as halite, salt is the mineral form of sodium chloride, meaning it is a crystal. Halite crystal possesses the powerful ability to transmute or transform dense and unharmonious energy into more usable, positive energy.

What you will need:

1 cup of Himalayan sea salt

3 white candles

A warm bath

Conscious awareness

Pour 1 cup of sea salt into a warm tub of water. Mix the water around with your finger while imagining it being charged with the energy flowing from your body. Light the candles and immerse yourself in the water. Begin to relax your body and focus your mind, inhaling and exhaling three times, slowly and deeply. Close your eyes and repeat the following affirmation as many times you feel is necessary: "Please cleanse my mind, body, soul, and spirit of all the negative energy I've accumulated to this day. I only want positive energy with only good intentions in my life from here on out."

When you are done repeating the affirmation, soak in the warmth of the salt water, imagining the negative energy being sucked out of your body by the powerful salt crystals and fresh nurturing bath water. Unplug the drain, allowing the water to subside. As the water is sucked down the drain, imagine any negative energy you want to eliminate being taken away with the bath water. Sit there until all the water has drained out of the bath. Allow the three candles to burn out on their own. Namaste.

HEALING EXERCISE FOR FORGIVENESS

Step 1 – Think of an experience in your life that continues to upset you and create feelings of resentment. Think about it until you have the idea clear in your mind.

Step 2 – Write your experience from your point of view, being as descriptive as you possibly can. Write it as if you are writing an excerpt in your journal, allowing yourself to get deeply personal. Try to feel every deep-seated emotion caused by the situation that is affecting your happiness and limiting you from experiencing forgiveness of yourself.

Step 3 – Write your experience as if from another person's point of view. If anyone else was involved, write what you think they might have been feeling. Put yourself in their shoes. If there was more than one person involved, write down what you believe each one of them was feeling. Be descriptive, taking as much time as you need to make it as clear as possible.

Step 4 – Write your experience from a completely different point of view, as if you are a reporter for a newspaper or magazine article. View the situation from a stranger's perspective, contemplating the situation as if you are reporting something for others to hear or read.

Step 5 –The next step might be kind of tricky. Find someone you trust who will not judge or criticize you, and read your experience out loud to them. This step will allow your experience to be set free into the Universe, which will in turn pick up on your vibrational energy, and begin helping you.

Step 6 – This is the final step. Gather up the papers you wrote your negative experience on and go outside. Find a safe, quiet place where you will not be disturbed and nothing will catch on fire accidentally. If you have a fireplace, this works best. Light the papers on fire with a match or lighter, allowing them to burn until they become ashes. As they burn away, imagine your negative experiences, melting away forever. You can also light the paper on fire above the toilet, and when they have burned to ashes, flush them away or throw them outside, against the wind. Continue doing this exercise anytime you want to find forgiveness in any situation you might encounter. This will aid you in reaching your recovery goals.

BREATHING EXERCISE FOR RELIEVING ANXIETY

Nadi Shodhana is a unique breathing technique that is beneficial for removing emotional blockages in the body, which in turn creates a calm and peaceful state of mind. Nadi is a Sanskrit word meaning "channel" or "flow", and is the subtle energy center running through the human body. Shodhana means "purification", therefore, Nadi Shodhana is a technique for clearing and balancing our energy centers, ensuring the pure flow of life force through the body. A few moments of this simple exercise each day assists in removing built-up stress and fatigue in the body by releasing anxious or restless thoughts in the mind. It also helps balance the left and right hemispheres of the brain, supporting balance between the logical and emotional parts of your personality. Nadi Shodhana's relaxing effect on the mind prepares you to enter a meditative state. It can be done before meditation to enhance the experience, or at any time to relieve stress and anxiety and bring you back into the present moment. When practicing this exercise, always remember the importance of moving through it slowly and mindfully to receive optimal benefits. This exercise should never be hurried or rushed. If at any time you feel short of breath, dizzy, or light-headed, simply stop and return to your normal breathing. Be sure to remain seated until the sensation passes. If you are wearing glasses, please remove them before doing this exercise.

Begin by finding a comfortable seating position, with your spine straight, your shoulders relaxed, and your left hand resting comfortably in your lap. With your right hand, rest the tips of your index finger and middle finger in between your eyebrows, in the location of your "third eye" chakra. Close off your right nostril with your thumb. Inhale slowly through your left nostril, as far as you can. Now, close off your left nostril with your ring and pinky finger, remove your thumb from your right nostril and exhale through your right nostril, all the way to the bottom of your breath. Inhale slowly and deeply now through your right nostril all the way to the top of your breath.

Close off your right nostril with your thumb, release your ring and pinky finger from your left nostril, and exhale through your left nostril all the way to the bottom of your breath. Repeat this pattern several times. This breathing exercise is an effortless continuous flow of breath with no controlled pauses.

HEALING BENEFITS OF GOLD

Gold has been known for its miraculous healing benefits since the earliest records of human civilization. Some people theorize that around 5,000 years ago, an advanced alien race called the Annunaki, landed where the Euphrates River meets the Persian Gulf, also known as Mesopotamia or modern-day Iraq. They speculate that the Annunaki were on a quest to find Monatomic Gold, a metal that repairs all bodily functions and stops the body from aging. In theory, the Annunaki created humans as intelligent slaves to help them find this precious metal.

The earliest records of the use of gold for medicinal and healing purposes come from Alexandria, Egypt over 5,000 years ago. The ancient Egyptians ingested gold for mental, bodily, and spiritual purification. They believed that gold stimulated the life force in the body by raising all levels of vibration, thus connecting humans with higher states of consciousness.

The Alchemists of Alexandria developed an "elixir" made of liquid gold. They believed that gold was a mystical metal that represented the perfection of matter, and its presence in the body would enliven, rejuvenate, and cure a multitude of diseases, as well as restore youth and perfect health.

As many as 4,500 years ago, the Egyptians used gold in dentistry. Remarkable examples of its early use have been found by modern archaeologists. Still in favor today as an ideal material for dental work, approximately 13 tons of gold are used each year for crowns, bridges, inlays and dentures. Gold is ideal for these purposes because it is non-toxic, can be shaped easily, and never wears, corrodes or tarnishes.

In medieval Europe, gold-coated pills and "gold waters" were extremely popular. Alchemists mixed powdered gold into drinks to "comfort sore limbs," which is one of the earliest references to arthritis.

During the Renaissance, Paracelsus (1493-1541) - who is considered the founder of modern pharmacology - developed many successful medicines from metallic minerals including gold. Considered one of the greatest alchemists/chemists of all time, he founded the school of Iatrochemistry, the chemistry of medicine, which is the forerunner of pharmacology.

In the 1900s, surgeons would often implant a gold piece under the skin near an inflamed joint, such as a knee or elbow. As a result, the pain would often subside or cease altogether.

In China, the restorative properties of gold are still honored in rural villages, where peasants cook their rice with a gold coin to replenish the mineral in their bodies, and fancy Chinese restaurants put 24-karat gold-leaf in their food preparations.

If metallic gold is divided into fine particles (sizes ranging from one to one hundred billionths of a meter) and the particles are permanently suspended in solution, the mineral becomes known as Colloidal Gold and exhibits new properties due to the larger amount of gold surface area available.

Colloidal Gold was first prepared in a pure state in 1857 by the distinguished English chemist, Michael Faraday. Many uses were found for the amazing solutions of "activated gold."

In the nineteenth century, Colloidal Gold was commonly used in the United States to cure the opiate, tobacco, and alcohol habits. Today it is used to reduce dependency on opiates, alcohol, caffeine, nicotine, and carbohydrates.

In the United States, as far back as 1885, gold has been known for its healing capabilities for the heart and improved blood circulation. It has also been used to treat arthritis continuously since 1927.

In July of 1935, Clinical, Medicine & Surgery had an article entitled: *Colloidal Gold in Inoperable Cancer,* written by Edward H. Ochsner, M.D., B.S., F.A.C.S. which stated, "When the condition is hopeless, Colloidal Gold helps prolong life and makes life much more bearable, both to the patient and to those about them, because it shortens the period of terminal cachexia (general physical wasting and malnutrition usually associated with chronic disease) and greatly reduces pain and discomfort and the need of opiates (narcotics) in a majority of instances."

Today, medical uses of gold have expanded greatly. It is used in surgery to patch damaged blood vessels, nerves, bones, and membranes. It is also used in the treatment of several forms of cancer. Injection of microscopic gold pellets helps retard prostate cancer in men. Women with ovarian cancer are treated with colloidal gold, and gold vapor lasers help seek out and destroy cancerous cells without harming their healthy neighbors.

Every day, surgeons use gold instruments to clear coronary arteries, and g

Gold has become an important biomedical tool for scientists studying why the body behaves as it does. By attaching a molecular marker to a microscopic piece of gold, scientists can follow its movement through the body. Because gold is readily visible under an electron microscope, scientists can now actually observe reactions in individual cells.

Some researchers are placing gold on DNA to study the hybrid genetic material in cells. Others are using it to determine how cells respond to toxins, heat and physical stress. Because it is biologically benign, biochemists use gold to form compounds with proteins to create new lifesaving drugs. Gold has been known for centuries to have a direct effect on the activities of the heart, and help to improve blood circulation. It is beneficial for rejuvenating sluggish organs, especially the brain and digestive system, and has been used in cases of glandular, nervous congestion, and lack of coordination. The body's temperature stabilizing mechanism is restored to balance with gold, particularly in cases of chills, hot flashes, and night sweats.

Colloidal Gold has a balancing and harmonizing effect on all levels of the body, mind, and spirit, by improving mental attitude and emotional states. It has been reported to promote a feeling of increased energy, will power, mental focus, and libido. According to many studies, colloidal gold increases mental acuity and the ability to concentrate. Colloidal gold is thought to strengthen mental function by increasing the conductivity between nerve endings in the body and on the surface of the brain. Gold is an all-natural mineral that is non-toxic, exhibits no interactions with other drugs, and is easily tolerated by the body.

The fabulous healing properties of gold are slowly but surely being rediscovered, as modern scientists and physicians uncover what the ancients seem to have known all along: That gold is indeed a very precious metal.

AYURVEDIC ART OF COLOR THERAPY

Surya Chikitsa is a 5,000 year old, ancient Ayurvedic practice that uses the seven colors of the chakras combined with the energy from the sun, to ensure the well being of *Pran,* or the vital energy instilling life in the body known as the soul. *Surya Chikitsa* is a natural line of treatment based on the belief that health of the body is directly related to the well being of *Pran*.

As we know, all energy required by living beings to survive is ultimately derived from the Sun. In a way, Sun is the life giving force. In Sanskrit, *Surya* means Sun and *Chikitsa* stands for treatment. Using the natural source of life giving energy received from the Sun to preserve and heal *Pran*, in turn heals the body.

The art or rather science of using the Sun's energy to heal our body was first developed in ancient India. Gradually this knowledge spread to Egypt, Iran, China, and in more recent times to the US and UK. During that era, scientific basis of *Surya Chikitsa* was not documented. The treatment stemmed from deep rooted religious beliefs. The knowledge was passed from one generation to the other by word of mouth. Only highly knowledgeable people, familiar with all the nuances of this line of treatment, specialized in it.

Although sunlight appears white, it is actually composed of the seven colors displayed in a rainbow. They are also the same colors as the seven chakras and are directly responsible for the correct and normal functioning of specific organs in the body. The imbalance of the quantum of the Sun's energy in our body leads to loss of vitality or weakening of *Pran,* in turn leading to sickness.

In the body, a particular color ray can act as a motivational force for a particular organ. If the quantum of color rays is higher or lower than the required average, then the organ will not function properly. This imbalance in our body manifests itself as a particular disease. If this imbalance is corrected, organ function will return to normal. Not only the organs, but all the cells in the body are also motivated by these colored rays to function in a normal way.

Sun Ray Therapy or *Surya Chikitsa* can be used to restore this balance. This therapy uses the natural source of life giving energy – the Sun – to heal and preserve *Pran* which increases vitality and eliminates sickness. Many chronic diseases people suffer from today are said to be cured using *Surya Chikitsa*. These include but are not limited to:

1. Insomnia, depression, tension, mental instability, degeneration of brain cells, migraine, Parkinson's, epilepsy, mental retardation in children
2. Mouth ulcers, boils on the edge of eye lids, pimples
3. Sinus problem, asthma, problems related to bronchi-trachea and lungs
4. Spondylitis, osteoarthritis, rheumatoid arthritis, sciatica pain, disabled knee joints, back-ache, lower back pain, pain at tail end of spine, any other joint pain.
5. Problems of the digestive system, worms in stomach, acidity, stomach ulcers

6. Paralytic effect, polio, muscular dystrophy
7. Fatigue, burns Sun Ray Therapy also offers many other health benefits such as:
1. It is a natural line of treatment having no side effects.
2. Root cause of disease is eliminated rather than merely suppressing symptoms of the disease.
3. Persistent, recurrent diseases are cured once and for all.
4. Potency of medicine does not reduce despite prolonged storage.
5. Body immunity is not developed by frequent or prolonged use of medicine.

Colors and their healing benefits:

- **RED:** regulates blood circulation, helps in digestive and breathing problems, stimulates cell growth, relieves constipation, creates alertness and self-confidence while decreasing lethargy and depression. Balances *Muladhara* or the Root Chakra.
- **ORANGE:** Stimulates the nerves and blood supply, increases thyroid activity, brings cheerfulness, increases confidence and joy while decreasing moodiness and feeling of insecurity. Balances *Swadhisthana* or the Sacral Chakra.
- **YELLOW:** Aids in constipation, eye and throat infections, soothes nerve pain, increases skin health while healing scarred tissues. Increases memory and charming personality while decreasing the tendency to be judgmental and fault-finding. Balances *Manipura* or the Solar Plexus Chakra.

- **GREEN:** Calms anxiety, depression, nervousness, inflammatory conditions and is beneficial to strengthen eyesight. Reduces indecisiveness, anxiety and claustrophobia. Brings positive energy and harmony with Nature. Balances *Anahata* or the Heart Chakra.
- **BLUE:** A calming color that brings tranquility and patience while lowering stress and negativity. Reduces bleeding, hair loss, body temperature, pain, helps heal burns, skin conditions, high blood pressure, aids as a stress relief, calms aggression and hysteria. Balances *Vishuddha* or the Throat Chakra.
- **INDIGO:** Purifies bloodstream, relieves mental stress, increases stability and rational thought and actions while reducing impulsiveness. Balances *Ajna* or the Third Eye Chakra.
- **VIOLET:** Treats emotional disturbances, stress, insomnia, eye and ear problems and headaches. Increases mental stability and rational thinking while decreasing impulsiveness. Balances *Shahasrara* or the Crown Chakra.

Here are some easy self-help Color Therapy techniques you can try at home:

Water Therapy: Buy some colored glass bottles with a lid or cork. Fill the bottle with 3/4 water and place in direct sunlight for 8 hours. Sip half a cup of this water three to four times a day. Do not refrigerate. For best results, keep the bottle in sunlight for three days before use.

Breathing Therapy: Place a colored glass bottle with lid in the sunlight for a minimum of two hours. Breathe in the air accumulated in the bottle.

Window Therapy: Cover your window with a colored gelatin paper of your choice and bask in the sunlight for a minimum of 10 minutes every day.

Oil Massage Therapy: Fill a colored glass bottle with the oil of your choice and charge it in the sun for 45 days. Each oil has a different characteristic color associated with it. For example, coconut oil should be kept in a blue bottle whereas linseed oil should be charged in a red bottle.

Color Bath Therapy: If you are unable to find a color bath therapy pouch, you can still relax in a bathtub, close your eyes and mentally visualize different colors moving around the seven energy centers to heal them.

Colored Fabric Therapy: Wear clothes of the color of your choice and sit in the sun for at least an hour.

Colored Candle Therapy: Lighting candles magnifies their color and the vibrations associated with the particular color are activated.

Gemstone Therapy: Dip the washed gemstone or crystal of your choice in a glass vessel full of water and place in the sun for a minimum of 2 hours. Remove the gemstone and drink the charged water.

30 DAYS TO FREEDOM MIRROR EXERCISE

DAY ONE • Pick a specific time to take your medication each day. After you take your first dose, stand in front of a mirror, where you can see your reflection down to your torso. Close your eyes, and set your intention for the day towards lasting recovery. Imagine yourself happy and free from the bonds of opiate addiction. See yourself with chains clamped around both wrists, and envision yourself breaking free. Inhale and exhale, three times, slowly and deeply. Look yourself deep in the eyes while repeating this affirmation 22 times: "I am very grateful I am no longer using opiates." Follow this exercise with a 20-minute guided meditation practice. You can find a variety of guided meditations on the internet for free. A meditation that has helped me tremendously in my healing and recovery process is "The Secret of Healing Meditations for Transformation, and Higher Consciousness," by Deepak Chopra.

DAY TWO • Take your medication and stand in front of your mirror. Close your eyes, and once again, set your intention for the day towards lasting and successful recovery. Imagine your mind cleared from all past conditioning and behaviors no longer serving you. Inhale and exhale, three times, slowly and deeply. Look yourself deep in the eyes while repeating this affirmation 22 times: "I AM very grateful I AM releasing all negative past notions and behaviors no longer serving me." Follow with another 20-minute meditation practice.

DAY THREE • Take your medication and stand in front of your mirror. By now, you should already be feeling noticeably better. Close your eyes, and set your intention for the day by imagining yourself free from the bondage of addiction. Inhale and exhale, three times, slowly and deeply. Look yourself deep in the eyes while repeating this affirmation 22 times: "I AM very grateful, I AM free from the bondage of addiction." Notice how your body feels as if the chains of addiction have become lifted. Follow this exercise with a 20-minute meditation practice.

DAY FOUR • Take your medication and stand in front of your mirror. Close your eyes and set your intention for the day by imagining your life filled with peace and love. Imagine green light energy beaming from the center of your chest, in the location of your heart chakra. Extend that love to everyone on Earth who is having a tough time ending their addiction to opiates. Know that this love will return to you tenfold. Inhale and exhale, three times, slowly and deeply. Look yourself deep in the eyes while repeating this affirmation 22 times: "I AM very grateful, my life has become filled with peace and love, and that I AM sharing this love with others." Follow this exercise with a 20-minute meditation practice.

DAY FIVE • Take your medication and stand in front of your mirror. Close your eyes, and set your intention for the day by imagining yourself connecting to the Divine Source that gave you life. Thank the Universe for protecting and helping you through all your struggles. Inhale and exhale, three times, slowly and deeply. Look yourself deep in the eyes while repeating this affirmation 22 times: "I AM very grateful, the Universe, has my back." Follow this exercise with a 20-minute meditation practice.

DAY SIX • Take your medication and stand in front of your mirror. Close your eyes and set your intention for the day by imagining your body healed from damage that might have incurred due to your drug use. Thank the Universe for protecting you and helping you find your way back into the light. Allow deep feelings of gratitude to penetrate through your heart and soul. Notice the feelings of warmth taking over your body like a warm blanket. Inhale and exhale, three times, slowly and deeply. Look yourself deep in the eyes while repeating this affirmation 22 times: "I AM very grateful, I AM healed from any damage caused, during my drug use." Follow this exercise with a 20-minute meditation practice.

DAY SEVEN • You have made it an entire week!!! You should be incredibly proud of yourself for surviving seven days without opiates. Take your medication and stand in front of your mirror. Close your eyes and set your intention for the day by sending gratitude to the Universe for helping you achieve this recovery goal. Inhale and exhale, three times, slowly and deeply. Look yourself deep in the eyes while repeating this affirmation 22 tines: "I AM very grateful, my path to recovery, is progressing more each day." Follow this exercise with a 20-minute meditation practice.

DAY EIGHT • Take your medication and stand in front of your mirror. Close your eyes and set your intention for the day by imagining yourself fulfilling a dream you have always had but never thought you could achieve because of your drug dependency. Hold the thought clearly n your mind's eye for a couple of minutes. Inhale and exhale, three times, slowly and deeply. Look yourself deep in the eyes while repeating this affirmation 22 times: "I AM very grateful each day brings me one step closer to fulfilling my dreams." Follow this exercise with a 20-minute meditation practice.

DAY NINE • Take your medication and stand in front of your mirror. Close your eyes and set your intention for the day by imagining all of your pain and guilt sucked out of your body by a natural energetic force. Inhale and exhale, three times, slowly and deeply. Look yourself deep in the eyes while repeating this affirmation 22 times: "I AM very grateful I AM free from all pain and guilt in my life." Follow this exercise with a 20-minute meditation practice.

DAY TEN • Take your medication and stand in front of your mirror. Close your eyes and set your intention for the day by imagining a protective bubble of blue light surrounding you. Imagine feeling the warmth from this healing protective energy encompassing your entire body from head to toe. Inhale and exhale, three times, slowly and deeply. Look yourself deep in the eyes while repeating this affirmation 22 times: "I AM very grateful I AM safe, I AM sound, and I AM happy." Follow this exercise with a 20-minute meditation practice.

DAY ELEVEN • Take your medication and stand in front of your mirror. Close your eyes and set your intention for the day by imagining yourself strong and healthy, able to withstand all temptations that could potentially lead you back down the wrong path. Inhale and exhale, three times, slowly and deeply. Look yourself deep in the eyes while repeating this affirmation 22 times: "I AM very grateful I AM growing stronger and healthier each day." Follow this exercise with a 20-minute meditation practice.

DAY TWELVE • Take your medication and stand in front of your mirror. Close your eyes and set your intention for the day by imagining yourself receiving rewards of abundance and prosperity for deciding to rid your life of opiate addiction. Inhale and exhale, three times, slowly and deeply. Look yourself deep in the eyes while repeating this affirmation 22 times: "I AM very grateful my life is full of new and exciting opportunities, leading me towards abundance and prosperity." Follow this exercise with a 20-minute meditation practice.

DAY THIRTEEN • Take your medication and stand in front of your mirror. Close your eyes and set your intention for the day, by imagining yourself helping others in need of support. Imagine yourself passing the information you have learned along to them, so they too can find the peace and contentment you now have in your life. Inhale and exhale, three times, slowly and deeply. Look yourself deep in the eyes while repeating this affirmation 22 times: "I AM very grateful I can pass what I've learned onto others so they too can achieve lasting recovery." Follow this exercise with a 20-minute meditation practice.

DAY FOURTEEN • You have been free from opiates for two entire weeks! You should praise yourself for coming this far. I cannot even express how proud I am of you! Take your medication and stand in front of your mirror. Close your eyes and set your intention for the day by imagining love and contentment surrounding you. Imagine it beaming out of you and then beaming onto everyone in the world who is in a desperate situation feeling like there is no way out. Imagine sending out rays of rainbow-colored light energy to guide them on the right path. Inhale and exhale, three times, slowly and deeply. Look yourself deep in the eyes while repeating this affirmation 22 times: "I AM very grateful my love energy is pouring out to those in need of support and will get returned back to me tenfold." Follow this exercise with a 20-minute meditation practice.

DAY FIFTEEN • Take your medication and stand in front of your mirror. Close your eyes and set your intention for the day by imagining your loved ones surrounding you with pure love, acceptance, and forgiveness. Mentally send them a message, letting them know how genuinely sorry you are for any pain you may have caused them in the past. Inhale and exhale, three times, slowly and deeply. Look yourself deep in the eyes while repeating this affirmation 22 times: "I AM very grateful I AM loved; people accept me for who I AM, and I AM forgiven." Follow this exercise with a 20-minute meditation practice.

DAY SIXTEEN • Take your medication and stand in front of your mirror. Close your eyes and set your intention for the day by imagining yourself living the life you have always wanted. Picture yourself in the house of your dreams and having the job you have always fantasized about. Inhale and exhale, three times, slowly and deeply. Look yourself deep in the eyes while repeating this affirmation, 22 times: "I AM very grateful I AM one step closer each day to living the life of my dreams." Affirm that you are worthy of making this dream your reality. Follow this exercise with a 20-minute meditation practice.

DAY SEVENTEEN • Take your medication and stand in front of your mirror. Close your eyes and set your intention for the day by imagining yourself surrounded by the energy of love and forgiveness. You can imagine this energy as a green light beaming out of your chest from your heart chakra. Imagine it surrounding your entire body and filling you internally from head to toe. Express deep feelings of love and forgiveness for yourself. Imagine all your shame and guilt melting away. Inhale and exhale, three times, slowly and deeply. Look yourself deep in the eyes while repeating this affirmation 22 times: "I AM incredibly grateful I AM releasing all feelings of guilt and shame. I now forgive myself and set myself free."

Affirm that you can love and forgive yourself and let go of the past. Follow this exercise with a 20-minute meditation practice.

DAY EIGHTEEN • Take your medication and stand in front of your mirror. Close your eyes and set your intention for the day by imagining yourself being comfortable, safe, and secure. Think for a moment about any conflicting situations affecting your life right now. Envision each problem crumbling into dust and blowing away in the wind. Inhale and exhale, three times, slowly and deeply. Look yourself deep in the eyes while repeating this affirmation 22 times: "I AM incredibly grateful I AM free from all negativity in my life. I AM safe, and I AM secure." Follow this exercise with a 20-minute meditation practice.

DAY NINETEEN • Take your medication and stand in front of your mirror. Close your eyes and set your intention for the day by imagining yourself surrounded by the gift of nature. See yourself on a hike enjoying the beautiful outdoors. Feel yourself taking in the beautiful energy nature offers. Imagine yourself breathing in the fresh air while the wind tussles your hair. Be grateful you have this wonderful gift from the Universe keeping you healthy and strong. Inhale and exhale, three times, slowly and deeply. Look yourself deep in the eyes while repeating this affirmation 22 times: "I AM very grateful I have the gift of nature keeping me healthy and strong." Follow this exercise with a 20-minute meditation practice.

DAY TWENTY • Take your medication and stand in front of your mirror. Close your eyes and set your intention for the day by imagining that you are one with the Universe. See yourself having the ability to manifest the life you have always wanted. See yourself happy and free from the enslavement of opiate addiction. Affirm that you are free. Inhale and exhale, three times, slowly and deeply. Look yourself deep in the eyes while repeating this affirmation 22 times: "I AM incredibly grateful I AM one with the Divine power that created me. I use this power for love, success, and generosity." Follow this exercise with a 20-minute meditation practice.

DAY TWENTY-ONE • Take your medication and stand in front of your mirror. Commend yourself for avoiding opiates for three entire weeks. Congratulate yourself and affirm that you are dependable and willing to continue your success. Close your eyes and set your intention for the day by imagining yourself succeeding at lasting recovery. See yourself running on the beach with someone you deeply care for. Envision yourself at a family gathering with everyone you love eating together and enjoying each other's company. See everyone smiling and laughing, making up for all the lost time. See how happy they all are! See everyone congratulating you, filled with genuine contentment in knowing that you are safe. Affirm that you are successful at your recovery. Inhale and exhale, three times, slowly and deeply. Look yourself deep in the eyes while repeating this affirmation 22 times: "I AM very grateful I AM successful at my recovery from opiate dependency." Follow this exercise with a 20-minute meditation practice.

DAY TWENTY-TWO • Take your medication and stand in front of your mirror. Close your eyes and set your intention for the day by imagining yourself filled with feelings of generosity and gratitude. These traits are fundamental for you to achieve success and happiness in your life. When you acquire them, you and everyone around you will benefit greatly. Affirm that you are generous and grateful for all that is and all that you have. Inhale and exhale, three times, slowly and deeply. Look yourself deep in the eyes while repeating this affirmation 22 times: "I AM very grateful I AM capable of expressing generosity and gratitude by helping others." Follow this exercise with a 20-minute meditation practice.

DAY TWENTY-THREE • Take your medication and stand in front of your mirror. Close your eyes and set your intention for the day by imagining the world void of addiction. See all the people suffering from addiction healed and happy. Envision yourself joining hands with everyone in unison, encircling the Earth. Affirm that together you are able to make a positive change for our planet. Be appreciative that you are able to play a part in this global unity that saves humankind from the misery and heartbreak associated with addiction. Imagine love pouring forth from your heart and encompassing the world. Inhale and exhale, three times, slowly and deeply. Look yourself deep in the eyes while repeating this affirmation 22 times: "I AM very grateful the world is void of addiction." Follow this exercise with a 20-minute meditation practice.

DAY TWENTY-FOUR • Take your medication and stand in front of your mirror. Close your eyes and set your intention for the day by imagining your body working towards perfect health. See yourself eating only nutritious foods and thinking only healthy, positive thoughts. Mentally send out love to all your internal organs and every part of your body. Affirm that you are accepting of healing and good health here and now. Be grateful to your body for all the good health you have had in the past. Be aware that every cell in your body is coherent and knows how to heal itself. Inhale and exhale, three times, slowly and deeply. Look yourself deep in the eyes while repeating this affirmation 22 times: "I AM open and receptive to all the healing energies in the Universe." Follow this exercise with a 20-minute meditation practice.

DAY TWENTY-FIVE • Take your medication and stand in front of your mirror. Close your eyes and set your intention for the day by imagining yourself as a young child. Try to remember one specific occasion you experienced as a child when you felt delighted and thrilled. If you cannot remember one, then try to imagine yourself as a small child experiencing joy and excitement. It could be a birthday, Christmas, or any other time when you may have felt completely loved and completely lovable. Hold that vision for a moment while you try and remember the emotions you felt. See yourself as you are now approaching the younger version of yourself with love and acceptance. Imagine reaching your hand out to the child within you and watching them grab hold of it. Now imagine the two of you embracing each other with feelings of forgiveness, compassion, and acceptance. Know that you are each beginning to heal and grow emotionally and spiritually as one unit. Express to your inner child how happy you are that you found each other. Let them know you will continue to keep them safe, protecting them from harmful, dangerous situations from now on. Tell them how sorry you are for causing them any pain. Inhale and exhale, three times, slowly and deeply. Look yourself deep in the eyes while repeating this affirmation 22 times: "I AM very grateful I AM able to love and accept everything about myself and my inner child is able to heal with me." Follow this exercise with a 20-minute meditation practice.

DAY TWENTY-SIX • Take your medication and stand in front of your mirror. Set your intention for the day by imagining yourself surrounded by positive energy and vibrations. Envision positive energy as the colors of the rainbow and see yourself surrounded by this magnificent multi-colored light. Imagine feeling rays of sunlight filling you with warmth and a sense of completeness. Affirm that you are always loved and accepted by Spirit and eternally protected by its Divine light. Inhale and exhale, three times, slowly and deeply. Look yourself deep in the eyes while repeating this affirmation 22 times: "I AM incredibly grateful for the infinity of life. Where I AM, all is perfect, whole, and complete." Follow this exercise with a 20-minute meditation practice.

DAY TWENTY-SEVEN • Take your medication and stand in front of your mirror. Close your eyes and set your intention for the day by imagining yourself surrounded by multi-colored light energy. See in your mind's eye magnificent rays in every color of the rainbow, beaming out of you and shooting upward towards the sky. Now imagine the colorful light shooting up past the sky and out into space. Picture these light rays directly connecting you to quantum frequencies in the Universe and know that this Divine energy is always guiding you to make the right choices. Affirm that you can do this anytime you feel lost or complacent. Feel the loving warmth and protection from the Universe filling your body and energizing your soul. Affirm that you are one with it. Inhale and exhale, three times, slowly and deeply. Look yourself deep in the eyes while repeating this affirmation 22 times: "I AM very grateful I AM one with the Universe and the Universe is always protecting me." Follow this exercise with a 20-minute meditation practice.

DAY TWENTY-EIGHT • Take your medication and stand in front of your mirror. Set your intention for the day by imagining yourself coming to a fork in the road. One path is dark and dismal, leading to addiction, misery, and destruction. The other road is bright and beautiful, leading to the entrance of a beautiful garden. Imagine the people you love waiting for you behind the gate. Now envision yourself choosing the heavenly path and entering the gate to meet your loved ones. See everyone happily enjoying their time together. Inhale and exhale, three times, slowly and deeply. Look yourself deep in the eyes while repeating this affirmation 22 times: "I AM very grateful I AM on the right path, and I AM moving in the right direction." Follow this exercise with a 20-minute meditation practice.

DAY TWENTY-NINE • Take your medication and stand in front of your mirror. Set your intention for the day by imagining yourself on top of a mountain. See yourself surrounded by the beauty of nature. The ocean is below with waves crashing against the rocks, but you are safe on top of the mountain. Imagine it is a beautiful, cloudy, windy day. The sun is shining down on you, big and bright, keeping you warm. Feel the warmth of the sun on your skin. Envision yourself, reaching your arms up toward the sky, feeling free and alive for the first time in your life. Picture yourself screaming at the top of your lungs, "I AM FREE!!!" Inhale and exhale, three times, slowly and deeply. Look yourself deep in the eyes while repeating this affirmation 22 times: "I AM very grateful I AM free from old limiting beliefs no longer serving me, and I AM moving forward in my life and in my recovery process." Follow this exercise with a 20-minute meditation practice.

DAY THIRTY • Take your medication and stand in front of your mirror. Set your intention for the day by gazing deeply at the reflection you see looking back at you. Notice how different you look since you decided to stop using opiates thirty days ago. Look deep into your eyes, seeing how bright and beautiful they look now that you have been blessed with Divine knowledge, keeping you safe and making you stronger. Be grateful that you got a second chance at life. Affirm that you did this on your own because you are a powerful spiritual being who can make good choices and live life to the fullest without the use of opiates. Commend yourself on the progress you have made and will continue to make. Inhale and exhale, three times, slowly and deeply. Look yourself deep in the eyes while repeating this affirmation 22 times: "I AM very grateful I AM making the best choices in my life, and I AM getting stronger and more consciously aware with each passing day." Follow this exercise with a 20-minute meditation practice.

You did it! You have been abstinent from opiates for thirty entire days! How do you feel? You should be so proud of yourself for such a huge accomplishment. Continue using the information you have learned to reach your full potential and help others to find freedom from opiate addiction. You are indeed a vision of light…as are we all!

30-DAY PERSONAL PROGRESS CALENDAR

1	2	3	4	5
6	7 ONE WEEK	8	9	10
11	12 TWO WEEKS	13	14	15
16	17 THREE WEEKS	18	19	20
21	22 FOUR WEEKS	23	24	25
26	27 FIVE WEEKS	28	29	30 YOU MADE IT! CONGRATS!

SELF-HELP RESOURCES

The following list of resources can be used to access information on a variety of different issues. The address and telephone numbers listed are for the national headquarters. Look in your local telephone directory for resources in your area.

In addition to the following groups, other self-help organizations may be available in your area to assist you in your healing and recovery for a particular issue you are having that is not listed here. You can search online, call a counselor or help line near you, or contact:

Substance Abuse and Mental
Health Services Administration (SAMHSA)
5600 Fishers Lane
Rockville, MD 20857
(877) SAMHSA (726-4727)
TTY: (800) 487-4889
SAMHSAinfo@samhsa.hhs.gov
www.samhsa.gov

National Institute of Drug Abuse (NIDA)
6001 Executive Blvd., Rm. 5213
Bethesda, MD 20892-9561
Parklawn Building
(301) 433-6245 (Information)
(800) 662-4357 (help)
www.nih.gov

World Service Office, Inc. (CA)
3740 Overland Ave., Ste., C
Los Angeles, CA 90034-6337
(310) 559-5833
(800) 347-8998 (leave message)
Zubsolv (Buprenorphine and Naloxone)
Bilingual Mint Tablets
(855) 982-7658
Email: info-us@orexco.com
www.zublov.com

Hay House, Inc.
United States Headquarters
PO Box 5100
Carlsbad, CA 92018-5100
(800) 654-5126 Ext 1 (United States and Canada)(760) 431-7695 Ext 1 (International)
www.hayhouse.com

RECOMMENDED READING

A Course in Miracles - Foundation for Inner Peace
Ageless Body, Timeless Mind - Dr. Deepak Chopra, MD
A Return to Love - Marianne Williamson
Bio-photons and Consciousness - Albert Popp
Civilization and It's Discontents - Sigmund Freud
Clean: Overcoming Addiction and Ending America's Greatest Tragedy - David Sheff
Constant Craving: What Your Food Cravings Mean and how to Overcome Them - Doreen Virtue, Ph.D.
Cosmos and Culture – Commentary on Science and Society - M. Gleiser
Creative Visualization - Shakti Gawain
Diet For a New America - John Robbins
Discovering the Child Within - John Bradshaw
Everyday Wisdom - Dr. Wayne Dyer
Excuses be Gone! - Dr. Wayne Dyer
Fire in the Soul - Joan Borysenko, Ph.D.
The God Code - Gregg Braden
Handbook to Higher Consciousness - Ken Keys
Healthy Healing – An Alternative Healing Reference - Linda G. Rector-Page, Ph.D.
Hermetic Sound Science – Egyptian Roots of Modern Sound Healing - A. Williams
How to Meditate - Lawrence LeShan
Life After Life - Raymond Moody, M.D.
Lifegoals - Amy E. Dean
Light is the New Black - Rebecca Campbell
Love Is Letting Go of Fear - Gerald Jampolsky, M.D.
Love, Medicine, and Miracles - Bernie Siegel, M.D.
The Magic of Believing - Claude Bristol
Many Lives Many Masters - Brian Weiss, M.D.
Minding the Body Mending the Mind - Joan Borysenko, Ph.D.
The Mirror a History - Melchior–Bonnet
The Morphine User – From Bondage to Freedom - Leslie E. Keeley
Opium a History - M. Booth

Opium and its Alkaloids - P.L.S. Jr.
The Opium Poppy – God's Own Medicine - S.W. Osler
Opium: Uncovering the Politics of the Poppy - Pierre - Arnaud Chouvy
Overcoming Addictions, the Spiritual Solution - Dr. Deepak Chopra
Peace, Love, and Healing - Bernie Siegel, M.D.
The Power is Within You - Louise Hay
The Power of Intention - Dr. Wayne Dyer
The Power of the Mind to Heal - Joan and Miroslav Borysenko, Ph.D.'s
The Power of the Poppy – Harnessing Nature's Most Dangerous Plant Ally - K. Filan
The Rainbow and The Worm – Dr. Mae Won Hoe
Real Magic - Dr. Wayne Dyer
Reinventing the Body, Resurrecting the Soul - Dr. Deepak Chopra
The Relaxation Response - Benson and Kipper
The Republic - Plato
Rockefeller Medicine Man – Medicine and Capitalism in America - E.R. Brown
Saved by the Light - Dannion Brinkley
Social: Why Our Brains are Wired to Connect - Matthew D. Lieberman
The Spontaneous Healing of Belief - Gregg Braden
Staying on the Path - Dr. Wayne Dyer
Thoughts of Power and Love - Susan Jeffers, Ph.D.
The Ugly History of Beautiful Things – Mirrors - K. Kellehe
Your Aura and Your Chakras: The Owner's Manual - Karla McLaren
Your Erroneous Zones - Dr. Wayne Dyer
Your Sacred Self - Dr. Wayne Dyer

Nothing ever goes away
Until it has taught us
What we need to know.
Life is full of lessons and teachings,
Sometimes cloaked in darkness,
Bringing us feelings
Of great sorrow, even despair.
At other times, however,
These very same teachings
Can liberate us,
Bringing us cause for
Joy and celebration.
When we embrace both the light
And the dark as our teachers,
We walk with courage,
With trust, with equanimity,
And finally with peace in our hearts.
The struggle disappears
And the quiet magic
Of the dance of life
Reveals itself to us
As unconditional love.

-THE BUDDHIST PAGE SUMAKHADRAN